THE YOUNG PERSON'S GUIDE
TO NOURISHING FAITH

THE YOUNG PERSON'S GUIDE TO NOURISHING FAITH

Aslı Kaplan

TUGHRA
BOOKS
New Jersey

Originally published in Turkish as *Gencin Yol Rehberi-2* in 2008.

15 14 13 12   2 3 4 5

Published by Tughra Books
345 Clifton Ave., Clifton,
NJ, 07011, USA

www.tughrabooks.com

Library of Congress Cataloging-in-Publication Data Available

Translated by Erkan Önler

ISBN: 978-1-59784-280-8

Printed by
Çağlayan A.Ş., Izmir - Turkey

CONTENTS

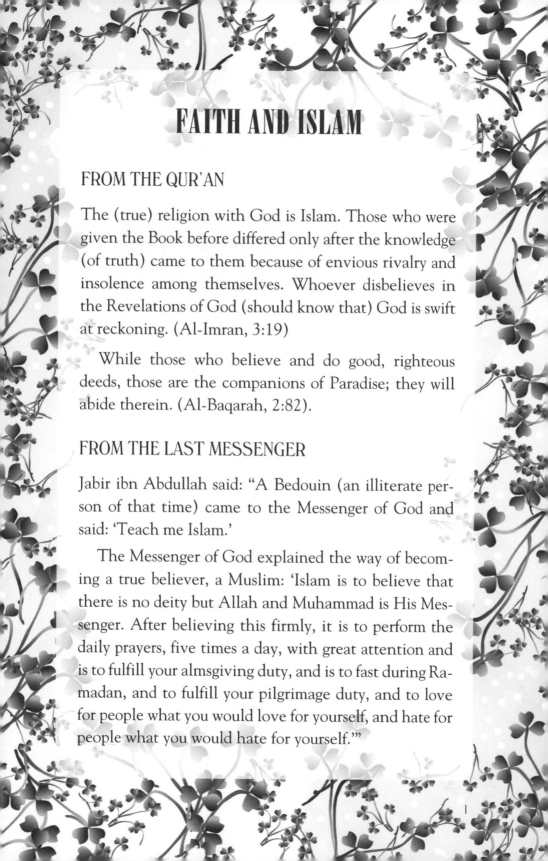

FAITH AND ISLAM

FROM THE QUR'AN

The (true) religion with God is Islam. Those who were given the Book before differed only after the knowledge (of truth) came to them because of envious rivalry and insolence among themselves. Whoever disbelieves in the Revelations of God (should know that) God is swift at reckoning. (Al-Imran, 3:19)

While those who believe and do good, righteous deeds, those are the companions of Paradise; they will abide therein. (Al-Baqarah, 2:82).

FROM THE LAST MESSENGER

Jabir ibn Abdullah said: "A Bedouin (an illiterate person of that time) came to the Messenger of God and said: 'Teach me Islam.'

The Messenger of God explained the way of becoming a true believer, a Muslim: 'Islam is to believe that there is no deity but Allah and Muhammad is His Messenger. After believing this firmly, it is to perform the daily prayers, five times a day, with great attention and is to fulfill your almsgiving duty, and is to fast during Ramadan, and to fulfill your pilgrimage duty, and to love for people what you would love for yourself, and hate for people what you would hate for yourself.'"

RELIGION IS THE SOURCE OF HAPPINESS

So far, people have always been happy when they have obeyed the rules of God. In contrast, when they have not paid attention to the teachings of the Prophets or the rules of the religions they have always suffered from a variety of depressions. The reason for this is very clear because it is a common fact that when everyone in a society behaves according to his/her own rules, an undesired confusion in the society becomes inevitable. If this sort of confusion occurs in any society, the weak and the poor are always the sufferers. People need the religion to prosper in both this world and the other world. The All-Knowing God created Adam as the first human and Prophet. As the heavenly religions explain who we are, from where we come and to where we go, in this respect, every society inevitably needs a religion.

Religions give the best answers to the questions for which we cannot find logical answers. We can obey God's rules thanks to religion. And it is religion by means of which we are able to stay away from the depression resulting from our lifestyles. We can also get rid of the feeling of being in a tunnel, the entrance and the exit of which are not clear.

It is religion by means of which we get the true information about the Owner of everything and the One who is always the Observer on us, surrounding the entire creation with His compassion. In addition, we can feel the real happiness even in our

hardest times considering the significance attached on us by God, the Most Merciful and the Most Compassionate.

We get a piece of very good news learning from the religion that the sufferings of life turn into good deeds if we are patient with them.

Undoubtedly, we all have the desire to live happily forever. It is God who gave us that desire. Thanks to religion, we all know that God will resurrect us after death, and God will also host us in Paradise in which we will live forever together with our best friends, and also in which we will be able to see God, in a way special to the other world.

Islam

Islam is the name given as a title to the religion sent by God through his Messenger. Islam has various kinds of meanings, the most important of which being obeying the rules of God. A true Muslim is a very dependable person about whom people feel reliance.

Islam is the final of the Divine religions preserving its originality. Its representative, which is Prophet Muhammad, peace and blessings be upon him, is the last Messenger sent by God. The last words about religion were uttered by God's Messenger. The previous Prophets spoke only for their own folks thus uttered the words "my folk" or "my public." In contrast, God's Messenger said "O people" or "O humanity," as mentioned many times in the Qur'an.

FOR ALL MUSLIMS

Having martyred the uncle of God's Messenger, Hamza, may God be pleased with him, Wahshi ibn Harb (literally the Savage son of War) came back to Medina. He escaped to Taif when Mecca was conquered. Meanwhile, Taif residents were going to the Messenger in order to convert into Islam. Now there was no place to escape for Wahshi.

Our Prophet sent a message to Wahshi in order to invite him to Islam. Wahshi answered saying: "O Muhammad, I have committed the big sins such as attributing a partner to God, killing innocent people and fornication, so how can you invite me to Islam? I don't think God forgives me."

Then God sent a verse of the Qur'an which says:

> Except he who gives up his way in repentance and believes (without associating partners with God), and does good, righteous deeds as such are those whose (past) evil deeds God will efface and record virtuous deeds in their place (and whose faculties which enabled the evil deeds He will change into enablers of virtuous deeds). God is All-Forgiving, All-Compassionate. (Al-Furqan, 25:70)

The Messenger of God sent Wahshi these verses upon which Wahshi said, "O Muhammad! Converting into Islam

and doing good deeds seem like a very hard job so I suppose I cannot make it."

Later, a new verse was revealed by God which says:

Assuredly, God does not forgive that partners be associated with Him; less than that, He forgives to whomever He wills (whomever He has guided to repentance and righteousness, either out of His pure grace or as a result of the person's choosing repentance and righteousness by his free will). Whoever associates any partner with God has indeed fabricated a most heinous sin. (An-Nisa, 4:48)

God's Messenger sent this verse to Wahshi.

Wahshi said: "O Muhammad! What is your opinion about me being forgiven? Since my forgiveness depends on God's will, I am not sure whether I deserve it or not."

Later, a new verse arrived which said:

Say: "(God gives you hope): 'O My servants who have been wasteful (of their God-given opportunities and faculties) against (the good of) their own souls! Do not despair of God's Mercy. Surely God forgives all sins. He is indeed the All-Forgiving, the All-Compassionate.'" (Az-Zumar, 39:53)

After our Prophet gave the news of the new verse to Wahshi, he decided to become a Muslim.

Meanwhile, some people also said to the Prophet: "O our dear Prophet, we did the same thing as Wahshi. Do the same conditions go for us, as well?" The Prophet said, "These conditions are acceptable for all Muslims."

WHAT IF HE TOLD SINCERELY

Osame ibn Zayd has explained: "The Messenger of God gave us the responsibility to introduce Islam to other tribes. We did so but some of them did not accept Islam and above all, said they wouldn't let us live in Medina. They were scattered around us. However, we caught one of them and he said 'There is no deity but God.' Though he uttered these invaluable words, we beat him murderously. When we came back to Medina we told the incident to the Messenger."

The Messenger said a bit angrily: "Who will be your helper on the Day of Judgment against these invaluable words of *tawhid*?"

I said: "He uttered these words because he was scared of our swords."

The Messenger asked: "Did you open his heart and check? What if he said it sincerely?"

He uttered these words so many times that I heartily wished I had not accepted Islam before that day of the beating incident.

FULL OF DONATIONS AND ALMS

Imam Ali once felled an unbeliever. Just as he was about to kill him, the unbeliever spat at him. Ali released him. When the unbeliever asked why, Ali replied: "I was going to kill you for God's sake. But I became angry when you spat at me, and so my intention's purity was clouded by my soul's inclinations. So, I did not kill you." The unbeliever replied: "I spat at you so that you would become mad and kill me instantly. If your religion is so pure and disinterested, it must be truth."

God's Messenger said, "The conversion of somebody into Islam is much more beneficial for you than giving a world full of donations and alms."

THE PRIEST IN THE MONASTERY

The Caliph Umar, may God be pleased with him, together with his friends, was passing before a monastery when he saw a priest with his long grey beard and who was also very old. Suddenly Umar gave way at the knees. He sat and started to cry at once. His friends were surprised and asked each other: "What happened?"

Yet, none of them knew the answer. One of them asked the caliph: "O Umar, what has made you cry so much?"

He, pointing to the priest in the monastery, said, "That priest is almost at the last steps of his life, yet, he still does not know Muhammad, the sultan of the universe, so I cry because of this."

The Caliph was crying for someone who he did not even recognize. He was crying because the priest couldn't find out the reality which was shining so evidently for anyone who was not prejudiced.

After all, it could have been no one other than Umar and the ones like him, who could donate half of their property without even thinking a second, and who could also cry for someone in a profound need of finding the truth of life.

FAITH AND UNBELIEF

If it were asked what the two things that are furthest to each other were, the answer would most probably be the title above. However, when you take the affairs around you into consideration in terms of your feelings, desires, conscience and blessings of God, then the two terms above are the closest things of each other in the world. There is a very fine line between them. Considering this fact, one should never condemn those who fall into the side of unbelief and always implore God earnestly to stay firmly inside the border of faith. Seeing the fact clearly, one should constantly pray to God to not skid his or her steps out of faith, not only for themselves but also for the others.

Because of the sins around us, in which one can easily fall and which may lead us away from the world of faith, we should always be cautious in order not to lose our straight way of faith. No one can be sure about preserving his loyalty to God, thus, being cautious is a necessity for all believers.

In this respect, nobody should trust themselves in protecting their faith. As believers, we always depend on God and demand His mercy and protection on us. Arrogance may undermine our faith in that it causes to trust ourselves exaggeratedly, thus closing our eyes to the reality.

A cautious person should always keep in mind the fact that people are profoundly in need of God, without the help of Whom we can't even take a short breath of air on Earth.

THE GUIDING LIGHTS

✿ Any calamity will be eased readily as long as one takes shelter in the strong faith of God.

✿ True freedom is to be a loyal believer of God.

✿ To be passionate is a necessity for publicizing the name of God and His religion.

✿ Not knowing God means knowing nothing.

✿ The only way of not becoming a servant or a slave to anyone is to be a loyal servant to God.

✿ Any conversation that does not lead us to God is deficient.

✿ Truth cannot be represented by inappropriate attitudes. Therefore we should be aware of how invaluable the truth of Divine is that we are representing.

✿ A true and sincere believer neither can deceive anyone nor can think of deceiving.

✿ A devoted believer cannot give way to despair.

✿ For a believer, hope means relying on God's infinite power.

✿ Arrogance is a sign of hypocrisy.

HONESTY AND VERACITY

FROM THE QUR'AN

God commands you to deliver trusts (including public and professional duties of service) to those entitled to them; and when you judge between people, to judge with justice. How excellent is what God exhorts you to do. Surely God is All-Hearing, All-Seeing. (An-Nisa, 4:58).

The true believers are only those who, when God is mentioned, their hearts tremble with awe, and when His Revelations are recited to them, it strengthens them in faith, and they put their trust in their Lord. (Al-Anfal, 8:2).

FROM THE LAST MESSENGER

Honesty

Our Prophet has said: "A loyal believer should always stick to honesty. Honesty leads one to such goodness that through which you can reach Paradise. If a person continues to be honest till the end of his or her life, he or she becomes qualified for Paradise.

A loyal believer should also stay away from telling lies since it puts you into a way which leads to deadly sins and eventually to Hell. If one continues to tell lies, after a certain time, he is indicated divinely as a sinful person and this status leads him or her to Hell eventually."

VERACITY

In the eleventh year of Islam, one night the archangel Gabriel descended to the world and took our Prophet to Masjid al-Aqsa on a mount named Buraq. Our dear Prophet became the prayer leader of the other Prophets, and saw Heaven and Hell during this journey. Later, our Prophet and Gabriel rose towards the spiritual realms. This trip, also known as *Miraj* (the Ascension), carried on the limit which is accepted as the upmost point of the created beings. Our Prophet continued his journey alone after this point. The Prophet met with God there in a way which is impossible to understand for us with our earthly criteria and comprehension. When the trip ended and our Prophet came back to Mecca, his bed was still warm.

Our Prophet told this his close friends in the morning then went to Ka'ba in order to announce the incident to the public. When the nonbelievers heard this, they ridiculed our Prophet whose telling lies had not been witnessed by anyone.

A short talk took place among them and they hurriedly went Abu Bakr to show him how an unbelievable incident befell the Messenger.

One of them said: "O Abu Bakr, you must know well how far the Masjid al-Aqsa is."

Abu Bakr said: "I know it takes more than a month."

The nonbelievers were very glad to hear this and they said joyfully and ridiculously: "A logical man thinks like you, of course. However, your friend Muhammad says he went there and came back over night."

Since Abu Bakr had a profound trust and belief in the Prophet, he disliked the approach of the nonbelievers and said: "If he told you this, then it was undoubtedly true, for I even believe him with more unbelievable matters , I believe he takes news every day from the heavens."

All the nonbelievers were flabbergasted and they said: "We cannot believe that you accept his journey to the heavens."

There was nothing for the nonbelievers to do except to leave the place and they did so. Meanwhile, Abu Bakr went to the Prophet promptly. There were many people around the Prophet but no one believed him when he mentioned about the *Miraj* incident. People again started to ridicule with him.

Abu Bakr approached them and said loudly: "Your every word is true, O the Messenger of God. May your *Miraj* be blessed!"

While Abu Bakr was shocking the nonbelievers with his words, he was invigorating the believers. Abu Bakr was nick-named as "the faithful friend" by the Prophet upon his unforgettable loyalty.

SAVED THROUGH LOYALTY TO TRUTH

Ka'b ibn Malik's words were as sharp as his sword. He was a poet. He could upset the nonbelievers entirely with his poems. He acknowledged our dear Prophet as the Messenger, and was among the first believers in Medina but he failed to join Tabuk military expedition.

The expedition was a very hard one because the Roman Empire was so powerful at that time that it seemed impossible to be overcome.

Ka'b narrates one of his memories of the day: "Since it would be a very hard fight, everybody was called for the war. It was regarded as extremely important by the Prophet. I finished my preparation like everyone. In fact, I hadn't made such a detailed preparation for any war before. When the army set on for the military expedition, I stayed back as I thought I would catch up with them easily. For so much time had I waited that I realized it was impossible for me to join the army. Days passed. There seemed no choice for me other than waiting. Each hour was like a day for me. No war took place and the army came back. The Prophet appeared on his camel and the native public, the children, women, old men, were all very happy to see him. The army stopped and the Messenger went to the Masjid to perform his traditional prayer after the military expedition. After his prayer, the natives visited him and the ones who had excuses for not joining the expedition declared them and all excuses were accepted by the Prophet. I could have done the same thing with them but I preferred not to lie and explained everything clearly. When we met, the Messenger gave me a meaningful smile and asked: "Where have you been?"

I told everything clearly. He turned his face and said: "You may leave"

When I went outside, my people surrounded me and they advised me to find an excuse.

I asked if there were any like me and they said: "Yes," and told me their names.

There were two other than me who both joined the Badr war and were also very glorious among the public. They were Murara ibn ar-Rabi and Hilal ibn Umayya. They both preferred my way and they didn't offer excuses.

The decision was made about us. Nobody would talk with us anymore. My two friends were always crying in their homes. I was stronger and I went to the Masjid regularly and I also passed time in the streets and public bazaars. Nobody talked to me. I waited so long just for a smile from the Messenger which never came for almost two months. Every day

I would return home with sorrow. The Messenger, the one whose face never ceases to smile, did not even once look at me with a smile. I would greet him, and gaze at his lips wondering whether they would move, but alas, there wasn't the tiniest movement or smile. 50 days passed. I visited my uncle's son one day. He was one of my best friends. I greeted him but he gave no response.

I asked: "Please tell me for God's sake! Don't you believe that I love the Prophet so much?"

I asked the same question three times and he answered in the third time, "God and His Messenger know better," and left.

I was absolutely shocked because I hadn't expected that answer. I started to cry loudly. While I was walking alone in the street one day I heard someone call me. The man approached me with a letter in his hand. The letter was from the sultan of Gassan. I was invited to Gassan by the king to live in his country. I was offered a free and entertaining life by him. I regarded this as a test from God. I threw the letter

into the fire. By the time someone called me after a morning prayer with good news, I had lost my ability to endure. I was forgiven by the Messenger. It was an unforgettable time for me so I prostrated. I thanked God. I went to the Messenger. I held his hand and he held mine. Nothing could have made me happier than touching his hand.

God had sent a verse about us:

> And (He turned in mercy also) to the three left behind and whose cases had been deferred (because they had not taken part in the campaign of Tabuk): (they felt such remorse that) the earth was too narrow for them despite all its vastness, and their souls became utterly constricted for them, and they came to perceive fully that there is no refuge from God except in Him. Then He turned to them in mercy, that they might repent and recover their former state (in Islam). Surely God is the One Who truly returns repentance with liberal forgiveness and additional reward, the All-Compassionate (especially towards His believing servants). (At-Taubah, 9:118)

After receiving this verse I said to the Messenger: "O dear Messenger! I was protected and saved thanks to my loyalty to truth. I would always tell the truth until the end of my life."

ALLAH KNOWS AND SEES EVERYTHING

Umar was checking the streets one night in order to be sure about the security of the public. He witnessed a conversation taking place between a mother and her daughter.

The mother was saying to her daughter: "My dear daughter, as you know we are desperately in need of money but our cows don't give much milk these days so we had better add some water to our milk."

The daughter answered: "I cannot believe you mom! You were not like this before."

The mother explained: "We could earn money in the past since we had a lot of milk. There is no other way for us now except adding water to the milk."

The daughter exclaimed, "But mom! Umar prohibited adding water to milk."

The mother said: "No way dear! We have to."

The daughter asked: "If Umar hears this, what will we do then?"

The mother said: "How can he hear us at this time of the night?"

The daughter explained: "Mom! Even though Umar does not hear this, what about God? God knows and sees everything."

The mother replied: "You are absolutely right my dear daughter. I appreciate your sensitivity. I also thank you for preserving me from committing a big sin."

Meanwhile, Umar was listening quietly to the conversation. He was impressed by the answers of the girl, her honesty, and loyalty to God. In a short time, Umar's son and the girl got married. Umar ibn Abdulaziz, who was one of the leading Islamic scholars, was the grandson of this girl.

RAIN CANNOT BE A REASON TO BREAK A PROMISE

Mehmet Akif Ersoy, a Turkish scholar and poet of the Turkish national anthem, knew the importance of keeping a promise. He was a devoted Muslim so he regarded breaking promises as unacceptable behavior.

He and his friend Eşref Edib promised each other to meet for lunch.

It was pouring rain one hour before their meeting time.

Edib thought that Ersoy wouldn't come to the meeting on such a rainy day.

So Edib left his home to visit one of his neighbors thinking the meeting was naturally cancelled.

In the meantime, Ersoy had already come to the meeting place. He waited under the rain.

The next day, after learning Ersoy had come to the meeting, Edib visited him to apologize. Mehmet Akif Ersoy said: "Only a death or a serious accident may be an excuse for breaking one's promise."

TRUSTING IN GOD

There was a man who was known by everyone in his village. He was famous for saying "God only knows why" after an incident befell him. While the other natives' sheep or goats were grazing free from danger that summer, his own donkey was killed suddenly without explicit reason. The man was not upset by his donkey's death and said: "God only knows why and there is bound to be a benefit for me in the end."

After a short time, his dog died. Again he was not upset by this. He said: "It is definite that there is a clear benefit for me in this."

After a short time, his rooster died suddenly. His neighbors said: "There is a bad luck in this." However, he was still determined that there would be a benefit in this. He said: "I trust God undoubtedly. He never gives human beings evils as long as they trust him and do the right thing. Even when people do bad actions, He mostly turns them into beneficial deeds."

One night, some bandits raided the village. As it was dark, they only hunted for the animal sounds such as a donkey and a roaster.

When they heard the animals' voices they went into the house and stole everything.

Almost all the houses were robbed that night except the man's.

His neighbors were all shocked and the man said: "No victory in the world should make you happier than as it is, and no loss should make you more miserable than as it is. Trust always in God and do never forget that God is the owner of all the property in this world. No incident in this world is occurring by chance. Everything has a meaning. As a human being, you should first take the necessary precautions including every detail you know, and then put your trust in God. And you should never be suspicious about the result which will always be in your favor as long as you trust in him taking all the precautions. At first, it may seem that some results are evil, but if you can wait patiently for the last step, you will see the benefits."

BELIEF IN GOD

FROM THE QUR'AN

(So, O people, refrain from concealing the truths and from disbelieving, and do not seek in vain a source of help and another refuge for yourselves. For) Your God is One God; there is no deity but He, the All-Merciful, the All-Compassionate. (Al-Baqarah, 2:163).

God it is Who has raised the heavens without pillars you can see, then He established Himself on the Supreme Throne; and He made the sun and the moon subservient to His command, each running its course for a term appointed by Him. He directs all affairs (as the sole Ruler of creation); He sets out in detail the signs and proofs of the truth and the relevant Revelations included in the Book, that you may have certainty in the meeting with your Lord (on Judgment Day). (Ar-Ra'd, 13:2).

(O my people!) Your only deity is God, other than Whom there is no deity. He encompasses all things in His Knowledge. (Ta-Ha, 20:98).

FROM THE LAST MESSENGER

The last Prophet said: "Undoubtedly, God doesn't put a person in Hell if he or she says '*La ilahe illallah*', there is no deity but Allah, just for the sake of Him."

God's Messenger said: "The one having these three things finds pleasure in his or her belief: To love God and his Messenger more than anything else, to love a person just for the sake of God, shivering with the fear of falling into disbelief after being saved from it by God."

DO NOT CRY MY DAUGHTER

The first things that the Prophet Muhammad, peace and blessings be upon him, did after his long journeys were to pray in the Masjid and then visit his daughter Fatima and his wives. After one of his journeys, Fatima met him at the door and embraced him by kissing his hands. Suddenly, she started to cry, and upon this the Messenger asked: "Why are you crying my dear daughter?"

Fatima responded: "O my dear father, I can see that you have gone pale in color and your clothes have become worn-out. This had touched me deeply."

The Messenger of God said: "Do not be sad my dear, because your father has been entrusted with such an invaluable religion that it would reach out to all parts of the world. Nowhere would be an exception. Some people would believe in this Divine religion and they would become people of dignity, unfortunately though, some would not accept it pushing themselves into indignity."

THE MOST HANDSOME OF MECCA

Mus'ab ibn Umayr was born into a family which was one of the richest of Mecca. Before he accepted Islam, he maintained a life full of luxury. When he was killed savagely in the Uhud war, he was lying in an old cardigan. He was cut into pieces by merciless swords. During his burial, a shroud could not even be found to wrap him, only the old cardigan. When his head was covered with a cardigan, his feet were left uncovered, and when his feet were covered by the cardigan, his face was left uncovered.

When the Messenger was informed of him, he ordered to cover his face with his cardigan and his feet with some wild grass. The Messenger approached him and looked at him compassionately and tearfully. He uttered the verse of the Qur'an:

> Among the believers are men (of highest valor) who have been true to their covenant with God: among them are those who have fulfilled their vow (by remaining steadfast until death), and those who are awaiting (its fulfillment). They have never altered in any way. (Al-Ahzab 33:23)

The Messenger stayed with Mus'ab and said: "When I first saw you in Mecca, you were wearing priceless clothes. No one in Mecca dressed as beautiful as you. But now you are lying in an old cardigan."

The Messenger was crying for him and suddenly, he turned towards the Uhud war field and said: "I bear witness that you will be resurrected as martyrs during the Day of Judgment!"

Then he turned his face to the people and said: "O my people, visit the martyred people of Uhud, come here and give your regards to them. They will hear whoever gives them regards and they will answer accordingly until the Day of Judgment."

HAVE YOU EVER THOUGHT?

Our body is a work of art consisting of approximately a hundred trillion cells. Our organs consist of cells undertaking the same duty in various numbers and in different forms. Indeed, trillions of cells without a mind, normally, cannot produce our organs without any conflict by just sharing the duties among themselves. Just as everything has a master, so there must be a Creator who brings many cells into existence and puts them in order.

Our nervous system arranging the operation of organs and controlling their movements in our body is a perfect structure made up of 80-90 billion nerve cells. Some 30 billion of these cells are available in our brain. Not all of the nerve cells are at the same length, some can even exceed one meter. If nerve cells were to be added end to end, they will reach at 760,000 km in length. This length is equivalent to the distance to the moon and back. As the perimeter of the world is approximately 40,000 km, the nerve cells in our body can encircle around the world 19 times when they are added end to end.

The nerve cells have a different feature from the other body cells: While body cells are reproduced by being divided, nerve cells cannot be reproduced in the same way as body cells. Namely, our brain consisting of nerve cells cannot grow day by day. If these cells did reproduce, our head would be as big as our body! Otherwise, by continually multiplying, brain cells would be pressed in the skull and it would be out of order after a period. Meanwhile, the operations of the nerve cells would be complicated and the balance of our body would be ruined and it would be impossible to live. However, God, who creates each organ in certain measurements and duties, has planned them in the most flawless way and has not wanted them to have a shapeless appearance.

There are about 340 muscles that enable our organs to work properly. As some muscles can perform some duties, our muscles perform 510 different duties totally. Arm and leg muscles are made up of red muscles. We can move our red muscles intentionally. However, our inner organs such as stomach, intestines, veins, lungs, and kidney have white muscles. In contrast to red muscles, these muscles work automatically. If inner organs were to work in our will, did you ever think what would happen? How would we make our blood flow in our body? How would we digest the food and make it pass to the blood? How would we make our kidneys work and breathe?

Our lungs are created to make the oxygen pass into the blood. The lungs are full of saccules called alveoli and these saccules are wrapped with capillary veins. The air, which we inhale, passes through the trachea and fills these saccules. As the oxygen pass to the blood through capillary veins, carbon dioxide is exhaled. The inner of our lungs must have enough width to breathe the air to meet the need of the oxygen for the trillions of cells in our body. That's why the inner surface of alveoli saccules has 55-100 square meter spaces. However, it is impossible for our lungs to know that we will inhale the oxygen and then exhale the carbon dioxide and that they should be wide enough to carry out this task. However, as the All-Knowing and Mighty God knows the needs of human beings, He has placed a very large space in a small area. He has also made us provide the needs fairly easy.

As the oxygen and food are necessary to reach cells, the blood which carries both needs to flow in our body properly. Namely, our heart works like a pump by shortening and loosening up to make the blood, as a miraculous liquid, flow in our body. The heart of an adult beats about two billion five hundred million times in a life. The heart beats continuously; it pumps five liters in a minute, 300 liters of blood in an hour and it pumps approximately seven tones of blood in a day.

The fact that the heart has red muscles is one of the most interesting features of it. While all of the red muscles work according to our will, the heart works without it. That is, the work of the heart does not depend on us and it works automatically. Let's think: If we had to control our heart, how would we live? How would we sleep and arrange the speed of the beat?

We have only mentioned about a few features but our organs have many features. These utterances show how perfect our body is. God has provided human beings with the most beautiful structures and planned their needs in great detail. Just like how a person likes his or her own work of art, God likes human beings created by Him without any defect or fault and with an elaborate work of art.

THE GUIDING LIGHTS

- Everything has a value to the degree that God attaches importance to them.
- God does not separate a beautiful one from the beautiful ones.
- Those who don't have a proper relation with God can't have a good relation with people, too.
- Disturbing winds always blow in the horizons of those who haven't got close relation with God.
- If we have a close relation with God thoroughly, He will make us successful with little things.
- Fine words find their real value with pure deeds.
- Blessings of God are better when kept secretly, but it may be disclosed to encourage others to do favors.
- God has reciprocity morals. He says; "Remember me; I will remember you; Pray and I will respond favorably to you!" Muslims should try to fulfill all the requirements of this Divine condescension.
- Mentioning God is an invitation to be remembered by God.
- Not to be conceited is an expression of virtue.
- To search for excuses of the fault is to multiply it.
- Bediüzzaman Said Nursi's works take people from blind imitation to unshakable belief.
- If we do not act for God's sake, our actions are not fruitful.
- To know and love God is His right and our main duty.
- We should wish God from God Himself again; and we should demand the consent of God. Consequently, a real Muslim is the one who can say: "Oh God! Accept me as Your servant, it is enough for me!"
- Each sin ruins one side of the human palace.
- Pray as much as your palms become numb from begging; I am certainly sure that God's response would be to turn the coal into diamond.

GENEROSITY AND CONTENTMENT

FROM THE QUR'AN

And who, when they spend (both for their own and others' needs), are neither wasteful nor niggardly, and (are aware that) there is a happy mean between those (two extremes). (Al-Furqan, 25:67).

Say: "If you possessed the treasures of my Lord's Mercy, still you would surely hold them back for fear of spending (in God's cause, and as subsistence for the needy)." Indeed human is ever grudging. (Al-Isra, 17:100).

FROM THE LAST MESSENGER

Generosity and stinginess

Our dear Prophet said: "A generous person is close to God, human beings, Paradise and far from Hell. A stingy person is far from God, human beings, Paradise and close to Hell. A generous but illiterate person is more valuable than a stingy devout person in the eyes of God."

Thankfulness

God's Messenger said: "Not thanking human beings is tantamount to not thanking God."

Contentment

Our beloved Prophet said: "How blessed is the one who has been granted with Islam and has enough of a living and is content with it."

Blessings

Our dear Prophet said: "When one of you considers a person more superior in terms of wealth and creation than himself or herself, he or she should turn his or her eyes to the one who is inferior in terms of wealth, health or creation. Such an attitude is essential not to look down on the blessings which God has granted."

WHAT A PROFITABLE TRADE

Anas narrates: "Abu Talha was one of the people among the Ansar who had very extensive date gardens. He loved the date garden which he called Beyruha the most. The garden was at the opposite end of the *Masjid* and our dear Prophet sometimes visited there and drank the water of the garden. When the verse *"You will never be able to attain godliness and virtue until you spend of what you love (in God's cause, or to provide sustenance for the needy). Whatever you spend, God has full knowledge of it"* (Al-Imran, 3:92) was revealed, Abu Talha went to our dear Prophet and said: "O my beloved Prophet! God said: *"You will never be able to attain godliness and virtue until you spend of what you love (in God's cause, or to provide sustenance for the needy). Whatever you spend, God has full knowledge of it."* I love my Beyruha garden the most among my property. I want to give it for the sake of God. I hope that God will accept it and take me to His Paradise. My dear Prophet! Use that garden in the way of God."

Our dear Prophet complimented him for those words and said: "What a profitable trade! What a profitable trade!"

RACE FOR THE SAKE OF ALLAH

The Muslims were about to set out for Tabuk Expedition. Before the campaign, the Prophet explained about the awards that Muslims will gain in the Hereafter. He also suggested rich people to bestow food and animals used for riding on the condition that they will take the payment in return in the Hereafter. Thus, Muslims began to bring their aids. There were even Muslims racing each other to donate for the sake of God. Umar thought he would get ahead of Abu Bakr this time because he had lost to him in giving donation for the sake of God once before, so he delivered the half of his wealth to our dear Prophet.

Then our dear Prophet asked: "Umar! What did you leave for your family?"

Umar said: "The other half of my wealth."

Abu Bakr then came and delivered his donation.

Our dear Prophet asked: "Abu Bakr! What did you leave for your family?"

Abu Bakr said: "I left God and our dear Prophet for them."

Abu Bakr had granted his whole wealth for the sake of God. Umar, who coveted by this magnanimity, cried and said: "O Abu Bakr! I swear that it is worth sacrificing my mother and father to you! You have been ahead of me in all races for the sake of good deeds."

GENEROSITY OF UTHMAN

During the Caliphate period of Abu Bakr, a great famine broke out in Medina. The people could not find enough wheat to make bread. The merchants from Medina who realized this situation invested their whole money in marketing. Uthman had sent a trade group to Damascus. He bought plenty of wheat. This amount could provide his needs to a great extent.

Upon this, the merchants immediately wanted to buy the wheat from Uthman. They proposed to give four *dirhams* (golden coins) as a price for a scale of wheat. However, Uthman found the price little and said "As far as I know, there are many merchants wanting to pay much more than you," he also said that he did not want to sell his wheat to anyone.

The merchants increased the price thinking they could convince him. However, Uthman did not change his attitude. Finally, they agreed to give seven golden coins for a scale of wheat. This was the final and the highest price. Nevertheless, whatever the merchants said, Uthman kept saying, "There are ones who will give much more than you" every time.

Some of them regarded his attitude as a behavior of opportunity-seeking and ambition to earn much more money. Uthman's attitude was considered shameful, especially when people were suffering from famine. Finally, they decide to tell Caliph Abu Bakr. They would

demand mediation from Abu Bakr. They clearly articulated the situation.

Abu Bakr listened to them and said: "Something's not right about this situation. I think you haven't really understood the intention and hidden purpose of Uthman. He is the son-in-law of God's Messenger and the friend of him in Paradise. He is not a man who perceives the needs of people as an opportunity and gets it out for himself. Indeed, his attitude has wisdom. Let's go and learn the matter from him."

Then they went to Uthman together. This time Abu Bakr explained all the developments. He asked him why he did not want to sell the wheat at that price.

Uthman said: "O Caliph of the Prophet! They want my wheat for seven *dirhams*. That is, they give seven to one. But does God not promise to give reward of up to seven hundred in return to each favor? Why should I sell the wheat to them while there is a more profitable trade?"

And Uthman gave the entire wheat out as alms to the Medina public. He made the poor and needy smile.

BEING THANKFUL FOR THE BLESSINGS

Ibn Abbas narrates: "Abu Bakr went to the Prophet's Mosque in the middle of a very hot day. Umar, who heard Abu Bakr come, asked: "O Abu Bakr, why are you outside at this hour?"

Abu Bakr said: "I could not stand starvation anymore so I went out with the hope of finding something to eat."

Umar said: "I swear that I am out for the same reason."

While they were talking, the Prophet came and asked: "What is it that has made you both go out at this hour?"

They said: "We are suffering from starvation."

Our dear Prophet said: "I swear the reason why I am out is the same reason as yours. Let's go."

They walked and came to Abu Ayyub al-Ansari thinking of finding something to eat. Abu Ayyub would normally put food or milk aside for our dear Prophet every day. But because the Prophet went there at a different time from the other days, he had fed his children with the milk and he had left to work in his date garden, which is very close to his house. When they arrived, Abu Ayyub's wife met them at the door and said: "Welcome my beloved Prophet and his dear friends, you gave us honor."

When the Prophet asked: "Where is Abu Ayyub?"

Abu Ayyub heard and recognized the voice and came immediately.

He said: "Welcome my dear Prophet and his friends! It is a great pleasure for me to welcome you. O my dear Prophet, this is not the usual time you always visit us. I hope nothing is wrong!"

Our dear Prophet said: "You are right, you spoke the truth."

Abu Ayyub, realizing the aim of the visit of this sacred group, went out and brought a bunch of dates consisting of dried, fresh and raw ones.

Our dear Prophet said: "I did not want three kinds, you should have brought only dried dated to us."

Abu Ayyub said: "O my beloved Messenger of God, I wanted you to eat three kinds of dates. In addition, I will sacrifice a goat for you to eat."

The Messenger of God said: "If you sacrifice it, do not sacrifice the one who is dependent on mother's milk."

Abu Ayyub said to his wife: "Knead dough and cook the bread. You cook bread well."

Abu Ayyub boiled half of the sacrificed goat and fried the other half. When the food was ready, the beloved Prophet and his two friends took a small piece of the meat and put it over his bread and said: "Abu Ayyub, take and send it to my daughter, Fatima. She has not eaten such things for days."

He did as the Prophet said. After the meal, the Prophet said "Bread, meat, and three sorts of dates…"

His eyes filled with tears and he continued: "I swear that we will certainly be interrogated by God from these blessings in the Hereafter."

While these remarks were difficult to swallow for the Companions, the Messenger spoke again and these words poured down from his lips: "When you get such blessings, you should say 'Bismillah!' After you eat, you should say 'Thanks be to God who has given us these foods and blessings, and have fed us with them showing His mercy towards us.'"

HE HAD DINNER AS A MUSLIM

Jehjah al-Ghifari narrates: "I came to Medina with the people wanting to become Muslim among my tribe. The Messenger of God was the leader of the evening prayer being performed at that time. After the prayer, he turned to his Companions and said: 'Take your friends with you to your houses.'

There remained no one but I and the Prophet. As I was a well-built and tall man, nobody took me. Finally, the Messenger of God took me to his home. He milked a goat for me and I drank the milk. He brought a pot of food and I also ate it. In total, I drank the milk which was obtained from seven goats.

Ummu Ayman said: 'May God starve the one who causes the Messenger of God to starve.'

Then the Messenger said: 'Never mind Ummu Ayman! He ate his food which was bestowed for him by God. God will give us our food.'

Next day we performed evening prayer with the Messenger of God leading us. The Prophet said again: 'Take your friends to your houses.'

Again, there was nobody who wanted to take me their home for the same reasons. The Messenger took me again as before and he milked only one goat this time. I drank it and I was full this time.

Ummu Ayman said: 'O my dear and beloved Prophet, is this the man whom we hosted yesterday?'

The Messenger said: 'Yes, he is. He had dinner as a Muslim tonight,'" implying that it was enough to satisfy his hunger with the milk of just one goat.

BELIEF IN THE ANGELS

FROM THE QUR'AN

The Messenger believes in what has been sent down to him from his Lord, and so do the believers; each one believes in God, and His angels, and His Books, and His Messengers: "We make no distinction between any of His Messengers (in believing in them)." And they say: "We have heard (the call to faith in God) and (unlike some of the people of Moses) obeyed. Our Lord, grant us Your forgiveness, and to You is the homecoming." (Al-Baqarah, 2:285).

God (Himself) testifies that there surely is no deity but He, and so do the angels and those of knowledge, being firm in upholding truth and uprightness: (these all testify that) there is no deity but He, the All-Glorious with irresistible might, the All-Wise. (Al-Imran, 3:18).

FROM THE LAST MESSENGER

Only God knows

Our dear Prophet said: "There are angels bringing every drop of rain and snowflake down to the earth and have no other duty. There is no space for four fingers to fit in the sky. There is an angel that prostrates everywhere. Only God knows the number of the angels."

Peace comes down

The Messenger of God said: "If a group of people come together to read and talk over the Qur'an in a house, certainly serenity (*sakina*) comes down and mercy covers them and the angels surround them. Moreover, God mentions about them to the *Muqarrabin* (those made near to God) angels."

A CALIPH ON THE EARTH

God said to the angels: "I will create a caliph on the earth."

They said: "Will you create a creature that will ruin the order and wreck carnage on the earth? Whereas we always praise You and always pray to You and always mention You."

God said: "I know many things which you don't know."

And He taught Adam all the names. After that, showing them to the angels, He said: "If you are consistent in your claims, then tell the names one by one."

The angels said: "O God! You are far away from all the deficiencies. We cannot know other than how You have taught us. You are the All-Knowing and You do everything with wisdom."

Afterwards, God wanted Adam to teach the names to the angels. After he taught them one by one, God said:

"I have told you that I know the secrets of the heavens and the earth, and I also know everything that you do secretly."

God said to angels: "Prostrate before Adam."

Remember (when) your Lord said to the angels: "I am setting on the earth a vicegerent." The angels asked: "Will you set therein one who will cause disorder and corruption on it and shed blood, while we glorify You with Your praise (proclaim that You are absolutely free from any defect and that all praise belongs to You exclusively,) and declare that You alone are all-holy and to be worshipped as God and Lord." He said: "Surely I know what you do not know." (Having brought him into existence, God) taught Adam the names, all of them. Then (in order to clarify the supremacy of humankind and the wisdom in their being created and made vicegerent on the earth), He presented them (the things and beings, whose names had been taught to Adam, with their names) to the angels, and said, "Now tell Me the names of these, if you are truthful (in your praising, worshipping, and sanctifying Me as My being God and Lord deserves). (In acknowledgement of their imperfection, and their perception of the truth of the matter, the angels) said: "All-Glorified You are (in that You are absolutely above having any defect and doing anything meaningless, and Yours are all the attributes of perfection). We have no knowledge save what You have taught us. Surely You are the All-Knowing, the All-Wise." (In order to demonstrate the superiority of humankind more clearly, God) said: "O Adam, inform them of these things and beings with their names." When he (Adam) informed them with their names, He said (to the angels), "Did I not tell you that I know the unseen of the heavens and the earth, and I know all that you reveal and all that you have been concealing?" And (remember) when We said to the angels: "Prostrate before Adam!" They all prostrated, but Iblis did not; he refused, and grew arrogant, and displayed himself as an unbeliever. (Al-Baqarah, 2:30-34)

ANGELS IN THE *MIRAJ*

God said to Gabriel: "My beloved Messenger is very upset in Taif. His body is wounded and his heart is broken. However, even in that condition, all he thinks is my sake. Therefore, go and bring my beloved to me. He will see the blessings of Paradise prepared for his followers and he will also see the torments of Hell prepared for his enemies. I will console him Myself and I will treat his broken heart Myself."

Gabriel found the heaven mount called Buraq waiting for this moment for 40,000 years. The affirmation of the oneness and uniqueness of God was written on the forehead of this white Buraq. Gabriel came to our Prophet and said: "O dearest Messenger, O the beloved of God! Do not worry about my visit. God sent you His regards. He is inviting you. This is such

a unique blessing that has been given to no other Prophet. Please, let's go."

The Messenger performed his ablution and then they walked to the *Miraj* together. They began to rise. 80,000 angels on their right side and 80,000 angels on the other side of the Messenger were accompanying him for this divine journey by holding a flambeau made of pure light.

Our Prophet met Adam in the first layer of heaven. The first Prophet greeted the last Prophet in a lovely way and prayed. Meanwhile, there were angels in deep reverence of God and they were saying: "*Subbuhun Quddusun Rabbul malaikati war-Ruh.*" (All Glorious, All Holy, Lord of the angels and the Spirit—Gabriel).

Our Prophet said to Gabriel: "Is this the way they pray?"

Gabriel said: "Yes. They have been praying in this way since they were created. They will stand this way until the

Judgment Day. I advise you to ask for this prayer for your *um-mah* from God."

When the Messenger wanted that prayer, this blessing was granted to us as the part of the prayer performed while standing up.

Our Prophet saw some people punished according to the greatness of their sins. When our Prophet asked Gabriel who they were, Gabriel answered: "They are the ones who haven't performed bowing and prostration properly in their daily prayers, those who have left Friday prayer and the prayer which is held by a community, those who haven't given one fortieth of his income distributed as alms, those who haven't felt compassion for the poor, those who have eaten anything forbidden by religion, those who haven't taken special care of something entrusted to them, those who have gossiped, those who have drunk alcohol, those who have engaged in perjury, those who have charged interest, those who have committed adultery and those who have objected to their parents."

A group of angels were praying in a bowing position in other layers and Gabriel pointed to them and said: "The way they pray is like this and it will go on until the Day of Judgment so wish this prayer from God for your *ummah*."

Therefore, this prayer was bestowed upon us. Our Prophet saw an angel sitting on a pulpit. There were shining angels on the right and oppressing angels on the left of the angel and they were working hard.

Gabriel said: "This is Azrael."

They went to the big angel and Gabriel introduced the Beloved of God to Azrael. Azrael greeted our dear Messenger and praised him: "Peace and blessings be upon you, the great Prophet who is the most superior among humans! Your *ummah* is more distinguished from the other *ummahs*. I behave to them softer than their own mothers and fathers for the sake of you."

The Messenger of God said: "Yes. I request this from you. My *ummah* is weak and I want you to take their souls with softness and without offending them, and I also want you to meet them in the most beautiful way."

The big angel made the valuable guest feel relieved with its explanation. After that, our Prophet and Gabriel went to the building called *Baytul Ma'mur* (the Pure House) made of scarlet ruby. Our Prophet became the prayer leader (*imam*) with Gabriel's offer and request, the angels of the seven heavens obeyed and they performed the prayer as well. Seeing the big community, prayers dropped from our Prophet's mouth: "I wish my *ummah* could pray with these big communities." God accepted the prayer and Friday prayer was given to Muslims.

The Prophet Aaron welcomed our Prophet on the fifth layer and greeted him. The angels here were in deep reverence of God and were standing upright, just looking at their toes. This prayer was also given to Muslims for the love of the last Messenger.

When Gabriel took our Prophet to a certain limit, Gabriel said: "My duty was up to here. I cannot go any further. If I take one more step, I will burn into flames."

Then Gabriel, who had come to the Prophet in different forms thus far, expanded his six hundred wings, and returned to his original form.

At this point a green Divine carrier, known as *Rafraf* appeared; this is a carrier that continually praises Allah and whose light is brighter and more overwhelming than the sun. *Rafraf* greeted the Messenger of Allah, peace and blessings be upon him. He mounted the carrier, which transported him through the seventy thousand veils, passing beyond the World of Spirits and the realms of the Divine Seat and the Divine Throne. Each time the Prophet passed through one of the veils, he heard a voice saying, "O Muhammad! Do not be afraid, draw nearer to Me."

On their way, *Rafraf* was unable to continue as the Prophet, peace and blessings be upon him, was getting nearer to the unparalleled proximity to Allah the Almighty—the nearness that is described as the *Qab Qawsayn*, or the "Distance between the Strings of Two Bows." Then suddenly a mount of white pearl appeared and accompanied the Prophet, peace and blessings be upon him, for the remainder of his journey.

When Allah the Almighty attracted the Prophet, peace and blessings be upon him, toward Him and the Prophet, peace and blessings be upon him, finally reached the unparalleled nearness to Allah, he bestowed his greetings to his Lord by saying: "*At-tahiyyatu li'llahi wa's-salawatu wa't-tayyibat*" (All the worship, prayers and goodness [performed by all living creatures through their lives] are for Allah.)

The Lord responded to the greetings of His beloved servant, saying: "*As-salamu 'alayka ayyuha'n-nabiyyu wa rahmatu'llahi wa barakatuh.*" (Peace be upon you, O [the greatest] Messenger and may the mercy and blessings of Allah be upon you too.)

The Prophet, peace and blessings be upon him, responded to his Lord's greetings: "*As-salamu 'alayna wa 'ala 'ibadil'llahi's-salihin.*" (Peace be upon us and upon the righteous servants of Allah.)

Then, Gabriel along with the angels of the seven Heavens began to testify in unity: "*Ashhadu an la ilaha illa'llah wa ashhadu anna Muhammadan 'abduhu wa rasuluh.*" (I bear witness that there is no deity but Allah, and I bear witness that Muhammad is the servant and Messenger of Allah.)

It was thus that the Muslims were bestowed with the honor of reciting this at-Tahiyyah prayer (that contains the greetings and conversation between Allah and His greatest Messenger) in the Prayer and their Prayer was deemed to be their journey of ascent to His proximity.

MACRO INFORMATION IN A MICRO LIBRARY

Let's think: There is a database that can fill one million ency-clopedia papers or a thousand books consisting of thousands of papers. If you put these books one after the other, the height of the books reaches 70 meters. If you write all of the information on these books one under the other on papers, the length of papers reaches from North Pole to the Equator. If you want to memorize all the information, a hundred years will be needed to finish it completely.

Is there such a database? If there is, what is it and what kind of a relation does it have with us? Maybe, you will be surprised but this database is present inside of us. Moreover, about 100 trillion databases are available in one adult person. Where is it? This information is in DNA which can be seen by magnify-ing thousands of times and only with an electron microscope. DNA has a perfect structure and it has been put in the cell nucleus perfectly. If we think of DNA as a library, it means that an adult consists of about 100 trillion libraries.

Then, what does all the information mean for us? The pro-gram of liveliness activity of our cells is hidden in the huge library which is small in terms of its structure. There are hundreds of ciphers belonging to every part of our bodies such as noses, our hair, and eyes. On the other hand, all the features building up our body are hidden in the ciphers of DNA. The fact that such a vast amount of vital information can fit into such a small area shows the Divine Knowledge, Command, Power, and Will.

The most important feature of DNA ciphers is that all the vital information in DNA belongs uniquely to us. Nobody has had the same DNA with another since the Earth was created. That is, there is nobody who looks the same, thinks in the same way with the others and behaves in the same way.

This situation also applies for twins who resemble each other identically. The thing making similarities between people is that about 99.9% of information is the same in DNA ciphers of everybody. Only the 0.1% part is different. This little difference generally makes people look different. Each person is created in a unique way. To create people in an amazing structure and form with a small difference is special for the All-Mighty and All-Knowing God.

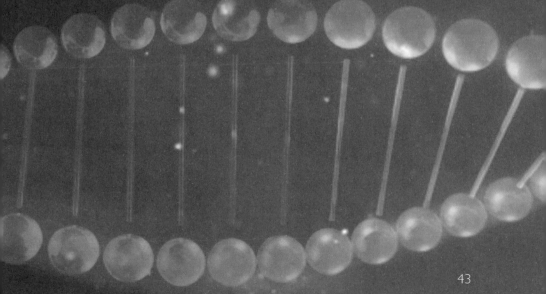

THE GUIDING LIGHTS

✤ Religion is so precious that it cannot be sacrificed for anything.

✤ If you can reach the pleasure of belief, you question yourself even for the thoughts passing through your mind.

✤ Before reading something to someone, it is more important to "read" him/her first.

✤ Setting the belief in your heart may be possible solely with the action of religious duty (a'mal).

✤ Compassion is the key which can open even the rustiest locks.

✤ Even a small amount of sincerity may lead to success.

✤ The greatest blessing that God bestowed upon us is sincerity.

✤ Being right does not necessitate being rude. Being moderate and modest adds rightness a valuable aspect.

✤ Even if you know you will be forgiven for your sins, you should always feel shame in the presence of God for them.

✤ We shouldn't mix being earnest with being sulky, our dear Prophet was both earnest and smiling.

✤ Not with words but it is with attitudes that every problem can be solved.

✤ Power of choice is one of the blessings bestowed by God.

✤ Satan uses the gaps or weaknesses in our personality in order to direct us to bad attitudes.

FAIRNESS, SELFLESSNESS AND MERCY

FROM THE QUR'AN

Do not confound the truth by mixing it with falsehood, and do not conceal the truth while you know (the meaning and outcome of what you do, and that what you strive to hide is true, and that Muhammad is the Messenger of God, whose coming you have been anticipating). (Al-Baqarah, 2:42).

There has come to you (O people) a Messenger from among yourselves; extremely grievous to him is your suffering, full of concern for you is he, and for the believers full of pity and compassion. (At-Tawbah, 9:128).

Were it not for God's grace and favor upon you, and His mercy, and that God is All-Pitying, All-Compassionate (especially towards His believing servants, what terrible consequences would such evils have caused in your community)! (An-Nur, 24:20).

FROM THE LAST MESSENGER

To the Compassionate People

Our Prophet said: "The merciful are shown mercy by the All-Merciful. Have mercy to those on earth, and the Lord of the Heavens will have mercy upon you."

Believers

Our Prophet said: "The parable of the believers in their affection, mercy, and compassion for each other is that of a body; when any limb of it aches, the whole body reacts with sleeplessness and fever."

Mild-Manner

Our dear Prophet said: "If a person is deprived of mild-manner, this means that person is deprived of the whole good deeds."

FARUQ

It was the time when our Prophet and the believers were hiding from the non-Muslims and when Umar ibn al-Khattab, may Allah be pleased with him, just became a Muslim. Umar came to the Prophet and said: "O Messenger of God! Are not we on the right path whether we are alive or dead?"

Our Prophet said: "Yes! I swear whether you are alive or dead, absolutely you are on the right path."

Umar said: "O dear Muhammad! As we are on the right way and they are on the wrong side, then, why do we keep our religion a secret? We have the right to announce it to everyone. The religion of God will be superior in Mecca! If our tribes oppose to us openly, then we will fight them. If they want to behave in a just manner, we will approve it."

Our Prophet then said: "We are too few."

Umar responded: "I swear that I have explained the essentials of Islam in all assemblies without fear. I swear that we will definitely appear openly."

After Umar's words, our Prophet went out of the home he was in, in two rows. Hamza was leading one row and Umar was leading the other row.

When they arrived at the Ka'ba, the non-Muslims were looking at Umar and Hamza.

Upon witnessing this sight, they were exposed to deep sadness and grief. After this incident, our Prophet named Umar as *Faruq* because he could distinguish the right from the wrong.

ONE DAY YOU, ONE DAY ME

When our Prophet announced that the Ansar and Muhajirun (the Helpers and the Emigrants) were brothers and sisters, he announced that Umar and Utban ibn Malik were also close brothers. Umar was affected by the favors of the last Messenger of God. Umar, who fulfilled all the requirements of every job and was able to do every job, was always helping his brother in religion under all conditions. They were going to the date garden and working there and coming back home together at night. They were going to do trade together.

Umar and Utban become much closer than the real brothers. They had heart-to-heart talks with each other, they would perform daily prayers together and go together to listen to our Prophet.

However, Umar, who loved the last Messenger of God so much, ever since the moment he kneeled down and sat to become a Muslim, wanted to be near our Prophet much more, he wanted to share the same place with him and to hear every word of the last Messenger of God and to learn them.

It became impossible for him to sleep because he was so busy with those thoughts. He decided to talk about his grief to Utban and said: "My brother, we are going to the last Messenger of God together. However, I want to learn more things from Him. I want to know the things that he told to our brothers before I became a Muslim."

Utban wasn't surprised of his words. He also wanted to be with the last Messenger of God. But they were also aware of the necessity of working really hard from then on. Utban suggested: "How about one day you go to listen to our Prophet and the other day I will go to listen to him. The one who goes to listen to him will share the things with the other."

Umar liked this proposal. While he was helping his friend, he would also learn the teachings of the last Messenger.

TAİF

Our Prophet and his adopted son Zayd went to Taif to announce Islam. He stayed there for about ten days and invited people to believe in the existence and uniqueness of God. However, after his meetings with the people in Taif, there was no one who wanted to help him. The people of Taif did not agree with his suggestions because they were afraid that the young people of Taif would become Muslims.

They said: "Go wherever you want but away from our land."

Then they mocked our Prophet and they put mischievous boys on two sides of the road where our Prophet would pass. These rude boys threw stones at him. At that time, Zayd tried to protect and hide him, and he sacrificed his own body to protect his. Nevertheless, the shoes of our Prophet were filled with blood. Zayd's head was injured. They took shelter in the vineyard of Utbah from Mecca. Our Prophet firstly and immediately cured the wound of Zayd. After he sat under the shade of a vineyard and had a rest, he performed his prayer and implored God: "Everything I do is just for your sake and all power belongs to you!"

Our Prophet and Zayd left that dangerous place after a short period of time. The Prophet, whose tender heart was hurt very deeply, was going towards Mecca inattentively. When he regained his consciousness, he realized that a cloud had shadowed him and he saw Gabriel after a short period of time. Gabriel said to our Prophet: "God heard the words that your tribe told you. God has sent a mountain angel for you to order him to do whatever you want for that tribe."

That angel greeted our Prophet and showed the mountain on both sides of Mecca and said: "Muhammad! I am the angel of mountains! Now wish whatever you want. If you want, I will gather two mountains and make them collapse over Taif."

The answer of our Prophet expresses the extreme level of patience, compassion and mercy he has even against those who insulted and declared him to be wrong: "No! I don't want them to perish. I want God to create people from that tribe who will pray Him and believe His uniqueness."

GUEST

On our Prophet's request, someone from the Ansar took a guest at his home for a meal. Upon arriving at his home, he said to his wife: "Is there anything to eat my dear?"

His wife's answer was negative. The man felt miserable but did not show his feelings and instead said to his wife: "Try to distract the children with something and make them sleep. When our guest comes and we all sit down to eat, blow the light out and so, in this way, he will think we are eating the meal together."

They sat and the guest ate the meal. However, the landlords starved that night. In the morning, this hospitable Muslim went to our Prophet and when our Prophet saw him, he said: "God accepted and liked your favor to your guest."

Upon this a verse was revealed:

Those who, before their coming, had their abode (in Medina), preparing it as a home for Islam and faith, love those who emigrate to them for God's sake, and in their hearts do not begrudge what they have been given, and (indeed) they prefer them over themselves, even though poverty be their own lot. (They too have a share in such gains of war.) Whoever is guarded against the avarice of his own soul —those are the ones who are truly prosperous. (Al-Hashr, 59:9)

BELIEF IN DIVINE BOOKS

FROM THE QUR'AN

This is the (most honored, matchless) Book: there is no doubt about it (its Divine authorship and that it is a collection of pure truths throughout). A guidance for the God-revering, pious who keep their duty to God. (Al-Baqarah, 2:2).

Those (illustrious ones) stand on true guidance (originating in the Qur'an) from their Lord; and they are those who are the prosperous. (Al-Baqarah, 2:5).

O you who believe! Believe in God and His Messenger (Muhammad) and the Book He has been sending down on His Messenger in parts and the (Divine) Books He sent down before. Whoever disbelieves in God and His angels and His Books and His Messengers and the Last Day, has indeed gone far astray. (An-Nisa, 4:136).

FROM THE LAST MESSENGER

The most effective word

Our dear Prophet told about the Qur'an: "Absolutely, the most effective word is God's book, the Qur'an. The most beautiful way is His Messenger's way. The worst deed is the deed which has been committed against religion. The promises given to you will be realized one day in the next world. It is impossible for humans to make God powerless."

Miracle

Our dear Prophet said: "God gave special miracles to all Prophets. The Qur'an was given to me as a miracle. Therefore, I expect to have the largest *ummah* in the Hereafter."

THE GUIDE OF
THE RIGHT WAY

The Qur'an is the book which was sent gradually to the last Messenger by God through Gabriel for approximately twenty-three years and the originality of which is impossible to change and the reading of which is a type of worship.

The Qur'an is a totality of laws which enlighten human beings with its perfect messages and broadens humans' horizons by taking all their physical, intellectual, and spiritual features into consideration.

The Qur'an is a revelation, that is, it is God's word. God sent the Qur'an and wanted it to take people to the light, to save them from ignorance, to take people to justice from tyranny and to lead people to the right way.

The Qur'an is a unique book which leads people to happiness via the shortest way with its infinite and unchangeable Divine principles. The Qur'an teaches people the necessities of being human, justice, and wisdom. In this sense, it is impossible to show another book which is equivalent to the Qur'an.

The Qur'an commands real justice, freedom and equality, good deeds, integrity and virtue and even compassion towards all beings.

The Qur'an is the unique book which forbids tyranny, injustice, ignorance, bribery, lying, perjury and laziness as well as indifference.

The Qur'an is the only book which effectively advises people to protect orphans and the poor and those who are exposed to injustice.

The most perfect lifestyle can be the life in which we feel the atmosphere of the Qur'an, a life other than this can never lead the people to happiness in this world and the next. All the excellent things appreciated all over the world are not different from the things which the Qur'an mentioned centuries ago.

The Qur'an is a Holy book which gives enough information about God and show God's uniqueness.

It is the only Holy book which tells and interprets the events in the universe and makes us learn a lesson from didactic events and leads us to gain God's acceptance.

LISTENERS OF THE QUR'AN

It was the first years of Islam in which our Prophet put up with a variety of difficulties during the daytime and also went to Ka'ba at night to perform prayers when everyone was asleep. The home of our dear Prophet had a different beauty at night. Our Prophet was reading the verses of the Qur'an loudly. Even though most of the people from Mecca were non-Muslims, they approached our dear Prophet's home secretly and they could not help listening to him while he was reading the Qur'an. There were some people who wanted to listen to him again and again. Abu Jahil and Ahnas who were the leaders of non-Muslims were several of the people who listened to the Qur'an secretly. They were too arrogant to listen to the Qur'an openly and they tried not to be seen by anyone at night while going to our Prophet's home to listen to the Qur'an.

They were listening to the Qur'an at each side of the home without knowing of the other. They sometimes came across while going to their home. However, they did not say anything to one another and they pretended not to see each another and moved towards their homes in silence. However, those few enemies did not accept Islam even though they were affected by those which they heard. They obeyed their own worldly desires and became arrogant. They were afraid of being blamed by the other non-Muslims or they thought of such useless excuses. In addition, they tried hard to stop other people from listening to the Qur'an which affected everyone who heard it.

However, Muslims did not leave communicating Islam and reading the Qur'an despite what the enemies did.

Our Prophet read surah *Al-Haqqah* at the Ka'ba and Umar ibn Khattab listened to him. Umar was a good fighter and a brave and courageous man. He was one of the people who found our dear Prophet's call meaningless and he lived according to the customs of his ancestors during the ignorance period. He began to listen to the verses at a corner in silence. He was deeply affected by the verses. He couldn't help admiring these divine words and he thought that the reciter was a real poet because these words could only be told by a good poet. Meanwhile, our dear Prophet was reading the verse: *"It surely is the speech (conveyed to you by) an illustrious, noble Messenger."* (Al-Haqqah, 69:40).

Umar was startled because our dear Prophet had known his thoughts and he thought: "Okay. He is an oracle at the same time as he knew my thoughts."

Our dear Prophet went on reading: *"And not a poet's speech (composed in a poet's mind). How little is what you believe! (It is so limited by the poverty of your souls and hearts.)"* (Al-Haqqah, 69:41).

Umar was deeply affected again and couldn't stop his tears and the stone deities he had worshipped his entire life came back to his memory. How would he leave them? How would he give up his religion after so many years? He wanted to get away from the effects of the words he heard, so he left there immediately. Umar came closer to Islam but, after a while, he was filled with the darkness of unbelief again. Those beautiful and influential words echoed in his ears again and again until he converted into Islam.

A JOURNEY TO ISLAM

Umar was moving with his sword through Mecca's streets very hastily. When he heard the number of people believing in Islam was increasing day by day in Mecca, he got really furious. He was walking very fast and saying: "I know what to do to you."

He encountered a man called Nuaym at that time. Even if Nuaym was a Muslim, he was hiding this. When he saw Umar, he asked: "Why are you in a rush? Where are you going?"

Umar answered: "To kill Muhammad!"

Nuaym asked again: "Why?"

Umar replied: "He is claiming to be a Prophet and everybody believes in him. People are going away from our idols. Moreover, the number of these people is increasing day by day. I won't be satisfied until I solve this problem completely."

Nuaym was startled by his words. He loved our dear Prophet very much and couldn't accept our dear Prophet being given harm. He must have persuaded Umar not to do so. However Umar was so decisive and angry that it was impossible to convince him. Nuaym tried to keep him busy and he said: "If you kill Muhammad, his tribe will kill you in return!"

Umar was not affected by this, because from the very beginning, he had accepted the risk of being killed. Nuaym wanted to inform our dear Prophet.

Again he said to Umar: "I heard that your sister and her husband became Muslims. For me, you should go talk to them first."

Umar did not believe it at first and said: "No, I don't believe you. You have made it up."

Nuaym suggested: "If you do not believe me, go and ask them yourself."

Umar threatened: "Okay, but if this is a lie, I will undoubtedly punish you!"

He decided to go to his sister Fatima and her husband. While he was moving very fast towards their home, he thought about whether the man spoke the truth or not and about whether his friends heard this or not.

Meanwhile, Nuaym came to our dear Prophet's home. At that moment, our Prophet was talking to his Companions. Nuaym told everything to our Prophet.

In the meantime, Umar kept moving speedily and he was in a state that he could not see the people around him because of his anger. Finally, he reached his sister's home. There were his sister, her husband and Habbab who was also one of the Muslims. At that time, Habbab was reading the verse: *"They ask you (O Messenger) about (what will happen to) the mountains (on Doomsday). Say: "My Lord will blast them into scattered dust."* (Ta-Ha, 20:105).

Umar tried to understand the verse. He approached the edge of the window and could hear the words clearly. The words reminded him of that night when he listened to the Qur'an at Ka'ba.

He knocked on the door with a huge bang. The people inside the house clearly guessed that it was Umar. Habbab concealed himself immediately. His sister and her husband wanted to hide the papers on which the verses were written. Because they obviously knew Umar would get angry if he saw them.

Fatima said worriedly: "Let's hide them. He will get angry with us."

Then they concealed them. Umar kept on knocking at the door and said loudly: "I am Umar, open the door!"

Fatima opened the door with fear. Umar entered in and went to his sister's husband and said: "There is a rumor about that you converted into Muhammad's religion. Is that really true?"

His sister's husband understood that Umar was aware of the verses that they read and said rhetorically: "Maybe, the religion we chose is better than yours."

Umar was furious and started to kick him. His sister interfered wanting to end this fight. Meanwhile, Umar slapped his sister on the face.

Fatima said: "Umar! The true belief is not your idols but the religion which Muhammad brought."

When Umar saw their determination for this religion, he understood that he could not persuade them regardless of whatever he did. He remembered the words that they read and said: "What were you reading? Show them to me."

Fatima hesitated and said: "We are worried that you may give harm to them."

Umar replied: "Don't be afraid. I will not give harm to any of its papers."

Fatima brought the papers. Umar performed the ritual ablution of the whole body and took the papers. The *surah* of Ta-Ha was written on the papers. Umar began to read it. After he read a few papers, he became calm and felt tranquility in his mind.

Umar said: "They do not resemble a poem or a word of human."

He looked as if he had been deeply influenced by it. His sister and her husband could not believe this. Umar was reading the paper in a calm way. Upon finishing, he said: "Let's go to Muhammad."

His sister's husband asked in a bewildered manner: "Why do you want to go to Muhammad? Will you give harm to him?"

Umar responded: "I wanted to kill him until I came here, however, now these verses have influenced me very much that I want to learn more from him."

Habbab, who watched the events from the place he hid, appeared immediately. Umar was bewildered when he saw Habbab because he hadn't realized that he was at home.

Umar said: "Tell me about the religion Muhammad brought and also about Muhammad himself."

Habbab mentioned about them and Umar was profoundly influenced by the words and he nodded by showing his approval of the words. He looked at Habbab and said: "I want to convert to Muhammad's religion. Take me to him."

Habbab was excited and said: "Good news Umar! You have found the right path. I hope you have had the blessing of Muhammad."

Now, Umar's thoughts were far different from the ones he had before he came to his sister's home. He had been very furious. However, now his heart was filled with tranquility. He wanted to go to God's Messenger immediately. Again he said: "Habbab! Let's go to Muhammad."

Habbab said happily: "Okay. Let's go immediately."

They set off and went to our Prophet's home. When they came close to the home, the Companions of our Prophet saw them and upon which they got nervous since they thought Umar would give harm to the Messenger. They immediately informed our Prophet and asked what to do.

Our dear Prophet said calmly: "Let him come."

The Companions said: "Okay, O Messenger of God."

However they thought about whether or not Umar had a hidden agenda. Hamza, famous for his heroic deeds, said: "Do not worry. If he comes for a good purpose, it's okay, but if he has a bad purpose, I will kill him with his own sword."

They opened the door. Habbab and Umar entered in and greeted them. Umar ibn Khattab, sat in front of our dear Prophet directly and said that he wanted to become a Muslim and he repeated the words: "I testify that there is no deity but Allah, and Muhammad is His Messenger."

Umar became Muslim in this way and the Companions were very happy and said: "God is the Greatest, God is the Greatest!"

At that time, Umar was a great power for Islam since he was a very influential man in Mecca.

The road leading Umar to kill God's Messenger, in reality, caused him to reach the main source of light. God accepted our Prophet's prayer. Before Umar became a Muslim, our Prophet had prayed very much for him: "O God! May You strengthen Islam through Umar ibn Khattab."

The fact that Umar became a Muslim was through the kindness of God and was through the blessings of the prayer of our dear Prophet.

IMPORTANT DUTY

God sent the verses of the Qur'an to our Prophet through angel Gabriel, one the four greatest angels. Gabriel read the verses to our Prophet and he made revelation clerks write these verses and many Companions learnt them by heart. Most of the Companions who preferred to memorize the Qur'an were virtuous and they also relied on their memories rather than writing the verses on papyrus paper. They also had to choose that way because writing was not developed much at that time.

Many people who memorized the Qur'an were raised as *hafiz* (a person who has memorized the Qur'an thoroughly).

Anyone who was powerful enough in terms of health and physical conditions fought in the war at that time. There were hafiz's among Muslims who died for Islam and Umar realizing this fact became anxious about the number of *hafiz*es. This is because those *hafiz*es were very important for Islam. He searched for a solution to the problem. He thought of a solution and decided to talk to the Caliph Abu Bakr about it.

One day when they were talking about the problems of the Muslim community, Umar said to him: "More than seventy *hafiz*es died for Islam in the Battle of Yamama. I fear that the other *hafiz*es will die in the other battles.

God forbid! We should take measures now. Let's gather the verses of the Qur'an and have it written into a book."

Abu Bakr was sharing the some anxiety with Umar, however he had another concern and said to Umar: "How will I do a job our dear Prophet did not do?"

Umar insisted and said: "My brother! This is a duty that we shouldn't hesitate about."

Then he articulated the matter with its details again and persuaded Abu Bakr.

Abu Bakr summoned Zayd to tell the matter. Zayd was one of the revelation clerks. After Zayd listened to Abu Bakr, he said to Umar: "Umar! How will we do such a job our dear Prophet did not do?"

Abu Bakr said: "I also asked the same question, but he persuaded me. We had better find a way to protect the *hafizes*."

Zayd thought about it and said: "I suppose you are right."

This important duty was given to Zayd by Abu Bakr with the insistence of Umar. Zayd achieved this duty after hard work. He gathered the verses of the Qur'an with great care and wrote them and handed it to the Caliph. So this was how the first copy of the Qur'an was prepared.

THE SURAH OF MULK (PROPERTY)

Ibni Abbas narrates: "One of the Companions set his tent on a grave unconsciously. I saw that the man read the *surah* of Mulk. After the man finished reading it, he went to our dear Prophet and said: 'O dear Prophet! I set my tent on a grave without being aware that I was on the grave. Then I heard that the person inside the grave repeated the *surah* till the end of it.'

Our Prophet said: 'That *surah* is protective and a savior, it protects from grave torment.'"

THEY WOULD GIVE UP

Ali ibn Abu Talib narrates: "When our dear Prophet was alive, the verses that came to him would always strengthen Muslims' belief and esteem towards God, and Muslims would immediately leave the deeds which were forbidden in those verses."

INHERITANCE

One of the Companions went to the public bazaar and said to the people: "I see you are all here while our Prophet's inheritance is being divided. Do you not need anything? What a strange thing! Why don't you go and take from his inheritance!"

Everyone ran to the Prophet's Mosque but they did not see any division of inheritance and they said: "We did not see anything like you said, only that someone was reading the Qur'an."

The Companion said: "That's right! Isn't the Qur'an our Prophet's inheritance anyway?"

AT ONE NIGHT

A young boy was taking the Qur'an lessons from his teacher. Those who realized the pale face of the young boy asked the teacher curiously: "This boy does not sleep to read the Qur'an during the night and finishes a complete reading of the Qur'an in one night."

The teacher said to his student: "My son, I have heard that you do not sleep at night in order to finish reading the Qur'an completely."

When the boy said that this was true, the teacher said: "My son, imagine that I am in front of you when you read the Qur'an tonight."

The boy did as his teacher desired and in the morning they spoke to each other.

Teacher asked: "Have you done what I said?"

Student replied: "Yes, my teacher."

Teacher asked again: "Have you finished reading the Qur'an completely?"

Student replied: "No, I could only read half of it"

Teacher said: "My son, imagine that a Companion, who listened to our dear Prophet reading the Qur'an, is sitting in front of you tonight. Pay attention, because the Companions listened to our dear Prophet when he was reading. Do not make a mistake."

The boy said "Yes" and he read the Qur'an again that night, yet he could only read one fourth of it. This time, the teacher said to him to imagine himself in front of our dear Prophet while reading the next night. The young student did as told but he realized that he could only read one section of the Qur'an. Finally, his teacher said: "My son, repent and ask God for forgiveness tonight, prepare yourself and imagine you are in front of God while reading the Qur'an."

The teacher waited for his student the following day but he did not come. When a man informed the teacher about the student's being ill, the teacher visited his student himself and found him crying. Upon seeing his teacher, the boy said: "My dear teacher, when I wanted to read the *surah* Al-Fatiha, I looked at my own worldly desire when I uttered the verse of *iyyakana'budu* (only for you we worship). I realized I did not feel the meaning of the verse, therefore, I felt ashamed of saying "*iyyakana'budu*", I said "*Maliki yawmiddin*" (The Master of the Day of Judgment) but I could not say "*iyyakana'budu*". Therefore, when I was bowing, the dawn grew light."

This young boy died one hour later. Afterwards, when his teacher visited his grave, he heard his voice: "My master, I am counted as alive in the presence of God. God rewarded me and He did not question me for my wrong doings."

SNOW

It was snowing for weeks and everywhere was white, the snow was being thrown into the air and it was scattered by the wind. There was a car stuck in the snow and this constituted a different color near the road. The car slid and went off the road.

There was a mother, a child and a father in the car. Halil, the father and the hero of the story, was waiting to hear a noise or to see a car, because their gasoline was about to run out and they could die in the midst of the white snow.

They were miles away from their home country. They had come to Russia just to educate the youth of the future. It was a very hard day for them. On the one hand his child was crying because he was burnt earlier that day after some burning oil from a frying pan accidentally spilt on his hand and they couldn't wait in the hospital for the complete treatment and had to leave, only getting some medicals for the burning because their other child was waiting for them at a neighbor's house and they knew he was crying. On the other hand, due to heavy snow and its difficult conditions they faced, his wife was muttering and saying: "Is it worth struggling for all of these things?"

Without permitting his wife to continue, Halil said: "Just be patient dear. Yes we are stranded. Maybe our gasoline will run out and we will freeze and die here. We should pray now and take the advantage of approaching God at this moment, because He is always with the innocent people."

Halil, in order to hide his tears from his son and wife, got out of the car and waited for a car that could help them. A lot of time passed but no one appeared. Halil was about to lose hope. He thought of his mother and father who knew nothing of the situation. He remembered his mother's soups which she made when he was ill. He couldn't stop his tears. However, he was never regretful for coming to a foreign country just for the future of young people. Suddenly he heard the noise of a truck which he ran towards and waved his hand. The man in the truck saw him and approached Halil.

He said: "My teacher, my teacher, you are Halil teacher, aren't you?"

Halil could not recognize this man and he ran to his wife and his child and said: "We are rescued."

Halil summarized the events to the man and the man said: "I am the older brother of one of your students. You came to our house and we talked to you. Don't you remember?"

His wife and his child were happy to be rescued but his wife began to mutter again and said: "When will our trouble end? When will we return to our own country and is it worth having difficulty here? I miss my mother and father very much."

The man intervened in the matter and said: "We weren't aware of peace and true belief until you came here. We were living in a swamp. You came here and lit the education flambeau and my brother became a different person by being positively affected from his teachers from Turkey. We discovered beauty and peace thanks to you. I ask you lady, is it not worth saving such people from the darkness and showing them beauty and peace?"

This question resounded with echoes inside the truck. Everyone was silent. It was as if the entire world was in silence. Emotions poured and the tears rained.

RETURN TO THE NEST

The animal realm has such beings that they constitute a model even for us with their own determination and perseverance. They set off on long journeys, travel long distances and cope with many hardships. Salmons are one of the most renowned and migrating animals. Their only goal is to return to their country which they left years ago. They pass through the route only once which they will use to find the place where they were born.

Salmons, which came out of eggs in the last periods of winter, spend their first days in the river where they were born. For a few weeks, they eat little fish there. Young salmons which have grown enough are ready to set off on a journey towards the oceans. Their mothers, which left them to the rivers when they were eggs, have already passed away.

They go on their routes until they arrive at the oceans. Salmons, which spend some years in the ocean, start to set off on a new journey when they become mature to bring forth young. Their only goal is to arrive at their own place in this journey which is much more difficult than the previous one. As they were inspired to leave their eggs in the rivers they were born, they set off on a journey to do this.

However, they time their journey well because they are supposed to arrive at the rivers on time to lay their eggs appropriately. And this can be realized by their knowledge of how long the journey will take and when they should leave the ocean to reach the river. Salmons arrive at the river on time, all the time. It is obvious that they are inspired by God.

The distance is so long that they are supposed to swim thousands of kilometers. After they go through the oceans for a long time, they need to find the place where the river they were born, flow. The second thing they do is to turn to the right side when the river separates in two parts. They do not take the wrong turning as they are inspired what to do. They find the rim of the river and go on their routes. However, the river current makes the salmon's journey difficult. Salmons which swim against the current have to pass the waterfalls on the opposite side by jumping meters in length.

Many researchers have held many studies in order to understand how salmons carry out all of these tasks. It seems obvious that the only explanatory answer is their special creation. Their noses have two holes and the water goes into one hole and then goes out of the other. When the water which has its own special smell goes into the nose of fish, recipients are warned chemically. Afterwards, this chemical warning is transformed into electric signals and sent to the central nervous system. Consequently, every smell is registered in the memory of the fish and the fish use this registration in their memory. They determine their route without confusion and turn to the route which lead them to the place they were born. When they arrive there, they leave their eggs to the place where their mothers left them. Coming out of their eggs, young fish start to live their lives which will end in the same place. Like all other salmons...

THE GUIDING LIGHTS

❖ As people need books, the books also need people who can represent well the books themselves.

❖ The Qur'an shows its beauty to those showing respect to itself, the people who do not show respect to the Qur'an have nothing which they can get from it.

❖ It is necessary to look for the Qur'an in our Prophet, and it is also necessary to look for our Prophet in the Qur'an.

❖ Religion becomes human nature as it is lived; so humans should follow it!

❖ Understanding and reading the Qur'an well depends on whether we learn the world and the age we live in.

❖ It is necessary to consider the Qur'an alive. If you show closeness to the Qur'an, it will also show closeness to you and so a spiritual link occurs.

❖ There is no equivalent thing to the Qur'an in terms of word choice according to the content.

❖ We should read the Qur'an by imagining as if we are reading it in front of God. We should say: "O God, we took these words from you and present them to you."

- To experience Islam properly, completely, and according to the Qur'an is the greatest blessing.

- Free-and-easy friends and environments should be regarded as the biggest threat.

- Even a rose has a thorn. The fact that a person is obsessed with the thorn results from the thorns in that person's own spirit.

- Saying "O the believers, believe" the Qur'an invites us to go over and refresh our belief.

- The major duty of the students of the Qur'an is to strengthen the feeling of slavery to God.

FRIENDSHIP, HYPOCRISY AND JEALOUSY

FROM THE QUR'AN

And (as the essential basis of contentment in individual, family and social life,) worship God and do not associate anything as a partner with Him; and do good to your parents in the best way possible, and to the relatives, orphans, the destitute, the neighbor who is near (in kinship, location, faith), the neighbor who is distant (in kinship and faith), the companion by your side (on the way, in the family, in the workplace, etc.), the wayfarer, and those who are in your service. (Treat them well and bring yourself up to this end, for) God does not love those who are conceited and boastful. (An-Nisa, 4:36).

FROM THE LAST MESSENGER

Hypocrisy

The last Messenger of God said: "Anyone who reveals the uncovered faults of another should know the fact that God will reveal the faults of that person. If one of you has hypocrisy, God reveals this hypocrisy to other people."

Jealousy

The last Messenger of God said: "Jealousy undermines recklessly every bit of good deeds, just as the fire uses up the wood. Alms eliminate bad deeds. Prayer (*salat*) is the light of a Muslim. Fasting is protection against the fire."

TWO PEOPLE FROM MY *UMMAH*

Anas narrates: "We were together with the last Messenger of God. He smiled and his molars were seen. When we asked the reason, he said: Two people from my *ummah* came to the presence of God. One of them said: 'O God! I have a right in this person: Take my share and give it to me.'

God said to the other one: 'Give his right back'

The man said: 'O God! I have no good deeds.'

God said: 'Look, this man has no good deeds. What do you say?'

The man said: 'Then, he can take some of my sins.'

Then God said to the right owner: 'Raise your head and look at the Heaven.'

The man said: 'O God! I see beautiful scenes, palaces, pearls. For which Prophet's *ummah* are these?'

God said: 'They belong to those who give their wages to me.'

The man said: 'No one can pay for them!'

God said: 'If you want, you can acquire them.'

The man said: 'How could it be?'

God said: 'If you forgive this man'

The man said: 'Then I will forgive him.'

God said: 'Take your friend and be accepted to Heaven.'

Then the last Messenger of God said: 'Be afraid of God, be afraid of God, and reconcile between friends. Pay attention, for God Himself reconciles between Muslims.'"

IF THEY HAD SEEN…

Abu Hurayra, may God be pleased with him, said to our dear Prophet: "God has some angels that walk among the public and seek the mentioning of God and worshipping assemblies. When they see a community dealing with the mentioning of God and worship, they call others: 'Come here, you will find what you seek.' All of the angels come and fill the gap with their wings up to the sky. Even though God knows them well, God asks them: 'What are my servants saying? What are they doing?'

Angels answer in a respectful way: 'O God! Your servants mention You by saying *Subhanallah*. They say *Allahu Akbar* when they think of Your works and read your names. They tell your uniqueness and greatness. They praise You by saying *Alhamdulillah* and they thank to you.'

God says: 'Have they ever seen Me?'

Angels reply: 'No, never.'

God: 'What if they had seen Me, what would they do?'

Angels: 'If they had seen You, they would perform much more worship and mention You much more, and they would serve You slavishly.'

God: 'What do they wish from Me?'

Angels: 'They wish Your Paradise from You.'

God: 'Have they ever seen My Paradise?'

Angels: 'No, never.'

God: 'What if they had seen Paradise I prepared for My loyal servants?'

Angels: 'If they had seen it, they would have wished Paradise insistently and they would have been more interested in it.'

God: 'What are they afraid of?'

Angels: 'They are afraid of Hell and they wish You keep them away from it.'

God: 'Have they ever seen Hell?'

Angels: 'No, never.'

God: 'What would have happened if they had seen it?'

Angels: 'If they had seen it, they would have been more afraid of it and would have tried to avoid it.'

God: 'I keep you as witnesses about their forgiveness. I have forgiven my servants who mention of Me day and night, who teach My beautiful names to others and who come together to gain my acceptance.'

One of the angels then says: 'There is a sinful person among them. That person was not interested in them and stopped by there for another purpose and intention.'

God: 'I have also forgiven him because they were such a community that a person among them cannot be unlucky.'"

FRIENDSHIP

A person who esteems, likes and supports his or her friends gains somebody who will back him or her in challenging and hard times.

A person's need for loyal friends is not in a subsidiary importance when compared with the other needs of that person.

The continuation of love and connection among friends depend on sympathy in suitable and logical actions and also self-sacrifice for each other. If there is no self-sacrifice in it, that friendship will be temporary and not a permanent one. The loyalty of a person to his or her friends may be indicated by his or her feelings and misery sharing with friends.

A real friend protects and backs his or her friend in hard times. Those who want many and loyal friends, should avoid unnecessary arguments.

Friendship should be very sincere. Those, who try to obtain it hypocritically, are mistaken all the time.

Those who are always in argument with others can have very few friends. If we want to have both loyal and many friends, we should abstain from unnecessary arguments.

THE CIPHER OF THE SCORPION

There were juniper trees along the river twisting in a series of curves. There were also willows whose branches were thrown into the air. There were also wolf howlings behind the mountains and the scents of the flowers.

Serhat found them too weird because he was acquainted with the apartment blocks, street corners piled with trash bins and the scent of diesel oil.

As it got dark, his fears were increasing more and more. Furthermore, he was chilled to the bone by the cold weather. When he heard a rustling sound, he directed the lantern towards there. He was trying to console himself in this way.

When the leader scout sent them to find the campsite, Serhat changed his way and thought that he could find the place himself. However, he could not reach there for many hours. When he realized his failure in finding the place, he sat under a tree hopelessly.

When he was sitting there, he remembered the conversation he had in the morning: "I'm right. The leader shouldn't have tried to match me with Levent, and what is more he considered me as a child. Above all, to the leader, this friendship will go on after camping and we should protect each other from the dangers all the time!"

The wolf howling took him out of these thoughts and immediately, he lit a fire with branch pieces. Then, he took his blanket and sat near the fire.

When he was watching the fire, he remembered the leader's words: "Look, Serhat! You and Levent are very good pairs. You should save each other in this small group."

Serhat said: "What's the good of it now?"

The leader answered: "You will correct your mistakes together."

Serhat said: "Do not take it lightly, in my opinion. Will Levent tell me my mistake?"

The leader said: "If a man sees a scorpion at the back of his friend, will he make a mistake if he informs him about it? The faults are like scorpions. The scorpions bite secretly but we cannot be aware of it. The warning of our friends is only a blessing and a favor to us."

Serhat covered himself with his blanket and heard a crackling sound but he could not look anywhere as he felt as if he was in the midst of a horrible nightmare.

The paces were coming closer and when he understood that the people pulled his blanket, he shouted: "Help! The wolves!"

He realized that they were not wolves and opened his eyes. The leader was standing there and Serhat stared at him for a long time. The leader said: "Serhat! Serhat! Calm down, there was no wolf here. Did you not notice me?"

The leader called his other friends: "Come! I have found Serhat."

After that, Levent and the others came and the leader said to Serhat by showing Levent: "Fortunately, Levent is your friend. Although he was very far away from the campsite, he came back to inform us that you separated from him; otherwise, we could not have found you."

Leader went on: "Come! Let's go back. We should not leave those in the campsite worried anymore."

When they were returning to the campsite, Serhat was laughing himself because he considered the crackling sound to be a wolf.

BELIEF IN THE PROPHETS

FROM THE QUR'AN

We granted Moses and Aaron the Criterion (the Book distinguishing between truth and falsehood,) and made it a (guiding) light and reminder for the God-revering, pious. (Al-Anbiya, 21:48).

Indeed We had, before this, granted Abraham discretion and his particular consciousness of truth, and We knew him very well (in all aspects of his character). (Al-Anbiya, 21:51).

We saved him and Lot (who believed in him), guiding them to the land (of Damascus, including Palestine) in which We have produced many blessings for all peoples. We bestowed upon him Isaac, and as an additional gift, Jacob (for grandson); and each We made righteous. And We made them leaders guiding people by Our command, and We revealed to them to do good deeds, and to establish the Prayer in conformity with its conditions, and pay the Prescribed Purifying Alms. They were Our servants devoted to worshipping us with all sincerity. (Al-Anbiya, 21:71-73).

And Noah, too. He had called out to Us long before (Abraham), and We answered his prayer and saved him and (those of) his family and people (who believed in him) from the tremendous distress. We helped him to safety from the people who denied Our Revelations. Truly, they were a wicked people, so We caused them all to drown. (Among those whom We made leaders were) David and Solomon.

The two were once judging a case regarding a field into which the sheep of some other people had strayed at night. We were watching and witnessing their judgment. We made Solomon understand the case more clearly. We granted each of them sound, wise judgment and knowledge (pertaining to the mission and in accordance with the time and conditions of each). And We subdued the mountains, as well as birds, to glorify Us along with David. It is We Who do all these things. (Al-Anbiya, 21:76-79).

And in Solomon's service We put the stormy wind, running at his command to carry him to the land in which We have produced blessings (for people). We have full knowledge of everything (with their true nature and all their aspects). (Al-Anbiya, 21:81).

And (mention) Job (among those whom We made leaders): he called out to his Lord, saying: "Truly, affliction has visited me (so that I can no longer worship You as I must); and You are the Most Merciful of the merciful." We answered his prayer and removed all the afflictions from which he suffered; and restored to him his household and the like thereof along with them as a mercy from Us and, as a reminder to those devoted to Our worship. (Mention also) Ishmael, Idris, and Dhu'l-Kifl (among the leaders). All were men of fortitude and patience. We embraced them in Our mercy. They were among the people of utmost righteousness. And (also mention) Dhu'n-Nun (Jonah). He departed in anger (from his people, who persistently disbelieved and paid no attention to his warnings), and he was certain that We would never straiten (his life for) him. But eventually he called out in the veils of darkness (formed of the belly of the fish, the sea, and dark, rainy night): "There is no deity but You, All-Glorified You are (in that You are absolutely above having any defect). Surely, I have been one of the wrongdoers (who have wronged themselves)." We answered His call, too, and We saved him from distress. Thus do We save the believers. (Mention also) Zachariah. Once he called out to his Lord, saying: "My Lord! Do not let me leave the world without an heir, for You are the Best of the inheritors." We answered his call, too, and bestowed upon him John, and cured his wife for him (so she was able) to bear a child. Truly, these (three) used to hasten to do good deeds as if competing with each other, and invoke Us in hopeful yearning and fearful anxiety. And they were utterly humble before Us. And (mention) that blessed woman who set the best example in guarding her chastity. We breathed into her out of Our Spirit, and We made her and her son a miraculous sign (of Our Power and matchless way of doing things) for all the worlds. So, this community of yours (which all the Messengers and their followers have formed) is one single community of the same faith, and I am your Lord (Who creates, sustains, and protects you); so worship Me alone. (Al-Anbiya, 21:83-92).

(O human being!) Whatever good happens to you, it is from God; and whatever evil befalls you, it is from yourself. We have sent you (O Messenger) to humankind as a Messenger, and God suffices for a witness.

He who obeys the Messenger (thereby) obeys God, and he who turns away from him (and his way), (do not be grieved, O Messenger, for) We have not sent you as a keeper and watcher over them (to prevent their misdeeds and be accountable for them). (An-Nisa, 4:79-80).

FROM THE LAST MESSENGER

The most precious word

Our dear Prophet said: "The most precious word is that: "*La ilaha illallahu wahdahu la sharika lah lahul mulku ve lahul hamdu ve huwa ala kulli shayin qadir.*" (There is no deity but Allah, He is unique, all property belongs to Him and praise belongs to Him and He is All-Mighty).

God's consent

The last Messenger of God said: "God speaks of a person leaving his or her home for His consent: If My servant leaves his or her home solely in order to struggle for the sake of Me, to strengthen his or her belief in Me and My Prophets, I promise that I will give My Paradise to him or her and I will reward him or her before re-arriving at their home."

Compassion

Our dear Prophet said: "Every Prophet has a prayer that God will accept. I keep it for my ummah to perform in the Day of Judgment. I hope that those, who do not attribute a partner to God, will gain it."

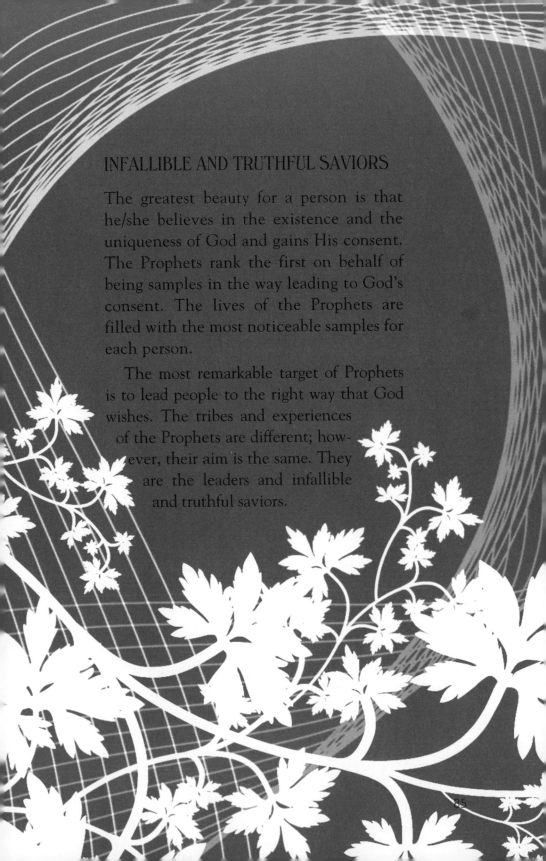

INFALLIBLE AND TRUTHFUL SAVIORS

The greatest beauty for a person is that he/she believes in the existence and the uniqueness of God and gains His consent. The Prophets rank the first on behalf of being samples in the way leading to God's consent. The lives of the Prophets are filled with the most noticeable samples for each person.

The most remarkable target of Prophets is to lead people to the right way that God wishes. The tribes and experiences of the Prophets are different; however, their aim is the same. They are the leaders and infallible and truthful saviors.

THE SULTAN OF THE PROPHETS

God, having infinite power, created the universe out of nothing in a perfect and outstanding way. God made the Earth the most ideal and beautiful place to live for all the beings. Afterwards, God sent His human beings to see the beauties, to taste the blessings and to know God Himself.

While God sent human beings to the Earth, He did not leave them ownerless and aimless. God sent His Prophets to introduce Himself to people, to tell people how to pray, to show the blessings of the world and the Hereafter. All the Prophets notified the decrees of God to the human beings, who are the Caliphs of God in this world.

God made some of those noble Prophets, who are the honors of humankind, superior than others. Our noble Prophet is the sultan of all other Prophets. As the other Prophets are the stars of the sky of humankind, our noble Prophet is the sun of that sky.

Therefore, God made our dear Prophet known to the other Prophets and wanted them to tell their own *ummah*s about our dear Prophet.

They kept their words and made their *ummah*s know the last Prophet who would come in the time during which the last judgment can be expected to take place. They also wanted to be an *ummah* of our last Prophet. However, they could not be an *ummah* of him as they were born before him. Nevertheless, they were honored by performing the prayer behind our Prophet in the night of the *Miraj*.

Our Prophet is the last Prophet but his soul was created before Adam's. If we compare humankind to a tree, our Prophet himself is the most luminous and perfect fruit, and the light of our Prophet is the seed of that tree. Likewise, when people asked our Prophet when Prophethood was bestowed to him, he said "When Adam was between soul and body."

All the Prophets from Adam to our Prophet made humankind ready for Islam and our Prophet's Prophethood.

All the Prophets, real scholars and sincere people witnessed his Prophethood. Moreover, God witnesses in the Qur'an:

> He it is Who has sent His Messenger with the Divine guidance and the Religion of truth that He may make it prevail over all religions. God suffices for a witness (for the truth of His promise and the mission of His Messenger). Muhammad is the Messenger of God; and those who are in his company are firm and unyielding against the unbelievers, and compassionate among themselves. You see them (constant in the Prayer) bowing down and prostrating, seeking favor with God and His approval and good pleasure. Their marks are on their faces, traced by prostration. This is their description in the Torah; and their description in the Gospel: like a seed that has sprouted its shoot, then it has strengthened it, and then risen firmly on its stem, delighting the sowers (with joy and wonder); (thereby) it fills the unbelievers with rage at them (the believers). God has promised all those among them who believe and do good, righteous deeds forgiveness (to bring unforeseen blessings) and a tremendous reward. (Al-Fath, 48:28-29)

We also say the Islamic confession of faith and pray to God to deserve to be the *ummah* of that glorious Prophet.

PROPHET MUHAMMAD
(PEACE AND BLESSINGS BE UPON HİM)

While our Prophet was the most perfect person of all human beings in terms of morality and attitudes, he was created perfectly in body structure as well. He was extremely handsome. He looked grand and those who looked at his face were filled with loving feelings since he was like the sun. Abdullah ibn Salam, after becoming a Muslim, said when he saw his face: "I swear that this face cannot belong to a liar."

Jabir ibn Samurah trying to describe that beauty uttered those words: "One night when there was no cloud in the sky and the moon was shining, I looked at our Prophet's face at first and then I looked at the moon. I found our Prophet's face more beautiful than the moon."

Our dear Prophet was of medium height. His complexion was rose-colored, with a mixture of red and white. His forehead was wide and his eyebrows were adjacent. There was a vein appearing between his eyebrows when he was annoyed. His face lines were plump but he was not fat. There was a red mark which was considered as seal of Prophethood between his two shoulder blades, his palms were plump, his arms were long, and his ankles were thin and gracious.

His teeth were shining when he opened his mouth. There were very slight gap between his teeth and his eyes were black and big. His hair was brown and it was neither straight nor curly. He usually let his hair grow long up to his earlobes. He combed them on both sides and he did not neglect hair care. When he combed his hair, it looked like the waves which storms make in the stagnant water.

His beard was thick and his eyelashes were curled and long. The space between his chin and lower lip was wide and a few white hairs in this part looked like white pearls. There were also a few white hairs in his hair.

Our dear Prophet's skin, which was very soft like silk, spread excellent scents around. When he sweated, sweat drops dripped like pearl on his forehead. His mouth smelled very nice. If a drop from his mouth dripped into a water well, very nice musk scents would spread around.

He walked rapidly and people could solely catch up to him by running. His voice was nice and resonant. He spoke very clearly and finely.

As Bera said; humankind had witnessed that kind of beauty only once and those who love him will be honored to see him and his beauty in the hereafter.

THE MORALITY OF OUR DEAR PROPHET IS THE BLESSING OF ALLAH

There are some nice traits such as patience, contentment, generosity, modesty, self-sacrifice and courage, which everyone wants to have in life. These attitudes make a person a real human. However, there is one person in human history who has all of these attitudes. He is our dear Prophet. The morality of our dear Prophet was bestowed by God. He was bestowed with the faultless and perfect attitudes from which we can take examples to ourselves. His morality is the pure one which God praised and the Qur'an taught. God sent Islam to lead people to the right path and when God bestowed the Qur'an, He chose our dear Prophet to show people how to apply the Divine principles. All of the beauties which the Qur'an mentions about can be seen in our Prophet's personality.

When the Companions of our Prophet wanted to know more about the morality of our noble Prophet, Aisha said: "Don't you read the Qur'an? His morality comes from the Qur'an."

Whatever job or level one has, everybody can find something as a model in Him. Our Prophet's life is an ideal model for us all in every respect. He said regarding this point: "I was only sent to complete fine morality." He taught us the connection between His level of morality and His duty in the world.

His morality was innate

Our Prophet's morality was innate. The compassion of our Prophet would spread around all of us. He always helped and saved the poor, spoke soft words and became warm towards people and he behaved humbly and in a tolerant way.

All his feelings were balanced

Our dear Prophet harmonized the opposite temperaments in human nature perfectly. He never gave up his mildness and mercy even in his hard times. While he thought hard of all the people to be saved, he never neglected his family. He spent most of his day in a state of worship and mentioning of God, his heart was devoted to God all the time while he never neglected his duty and the public. He did not isolate himself from the world. He thought of God's approval in his every deed. He forgave all the malicious actions held to him. He did not think to take revenge for himself.

He was the most fearful of God

As our Prophet was the most superior of all the creatures, he knew God better than anyone and thus was fearful of God. While God saved him from sins, our Prophet prayed and vowed continuously. He slept in the early hours of the night and he prayed in the late hours. He performed his prayer so much and so long that his feet would get swollen.

When one asked, "O God's Messenger, though all your sins have been forgiven and you are innocent, why do you go through so much trouble for your worship?" he answered, "Shall I not be a thankful servant of God?"

He had the greatest humility

Our dear Prophet had the most perfect humility and modesty. While he was praised by God in the Qur'an many times, he did not profit from his Prophethood privilege and he did not accept himself more superior than others. When God set him free to choose to be a king-like Prophet or a human Prophet, he chose to be a human Prophet. Hence, Archangel Israfil said, "Surely God bestowed that trait to you as you behaved humbly. You are the master of the people in the Judgment Day. The earth will be split and people will come out of their graves and you are the one who will intercede first."

The one who saw him for the first time got excited

Any person who came to our Prophet started to shiver by his Prophethood's grandeur. When our Prophet saw the state of man, he said, "Pull yourself together, I am not a ruler. I am only the son of a woman who ate dried salty bread in a Quraysh tribe." Actually, the one who saw him for the first time would be excited. However, when people saw his compassion and smile on his face, they felt relieved and when they talked to him, the fear would turn into love. Our dear Prophet behaved equally to everyone and he never underestimated anyone owing to their lifestyles or poverty. He fulfilled what the weak people wanted.

He did his own tasks himself

Our dear Prophet did not want other people to be in service of him and did not want to be a burden on anyone. He used to patch his clothes, repair his shoes, heat the water for ritual ablution, go to the bazaar and buy whatever he needed and bring them home by himself. One day, Amir ibn Rebia and our Prophet were going to the mosque and the string of our master's shoes was untied and immediately Ibn Rebia wanted to tie it but our master drew his foot and said: "This means to have the other serve. I do not like having other people serve."

He had a simple life

Our dear Prophet had an extremely modest and simple life in his home and family. He sometimes helped his wives with the house chores, he used to sweep the floors, he used to tie and feed his camel, milk the sheep, do the shopping and carry items. Neither did he isolate himself from others nor did people prepare his meals for him. He sat on the floor and ate his meal there.

He was the most mild-mannered

He was the most mild-mannered after and before his Prophethood. He was the least furious, the most content and the most merciful to all the people. He did not think to take revenge because of the malicious actions held to him. When he tried to tell the orders of God, the Quraysh unbelievers insulted and teased him and put thorns on his way and threw filth to him. Moreover, they tried to make him angry by saying magician, oracle, and poet; however, he endured all of them and he was calm, tolerant and patient.

He never broke anyone's heart

He always behaved softly to those who served him and never got angry with them and never broke their hearts.

When they did not do what he said, he only asked the reason why they did not do it, softly and kindly. Anas ibn Malik who served him for years told one of his memories: "Our Prophet sent me somewhere. I went out and called in children who played on the street. I joined them and began to play forgetting my duty. After that, our Prophet came and held my head. I looked at him and he smiled: "My little Anas, did you go to the place I said?" and I said, "I am going now, my dear Prophet."

He was innocent and shy

Our dear Prophet was the most superior in terms of morality and virtue and the shiest one among people. He never looked at shameful things. He avoided to reveal the mistakes of people, he never reproached people sharply for their mistakes and thus he saved the love and respect relation between himself and that person. When he was informed of the bad deeds someone did, he never said: "Why does that person do or say so?" In general terms, he said: "Why do people do or say so?" Hence, he protected that person from his or her name being revealed among the public. He never said ill-mannered remarks and he did not attempt to do such a thing. He never spoke so loudly that people could be disturbed. He always behaved tolerantly. When he had to tell what he did not like, he told it indirectly. It was his shyness that kept him away from staring at anyone in a humiliating way.

There was nobody as compassionate as he was

Compassion and mercy were like a mirror of our Prophet's eminent personality. There has been nobody as merciful, compassionate, and sensitive as him. Those who were the closest to our Prophet's heart and receivers of great mercy were the poor and the homeless. He saved the poor all the time and showed concern for them so much that they would forget the oppression and vileness of poverty.

When he saw people gathering in different parts of the society, he firstly went to the poor and sat with them. He used to warn the people who felt more superior to the poor and homeless people of the community and told that people of every level needed each other continuously.

There was a poor woman cleaning the small mosque of our dear Prophet. When our Prophet did not see her for a few days in succession, he asked where she was. People said that she died. Nobody considered her death important enough to inform our Prophet about it. Our Prophet got upset and asked: "You were supposed to inform me about it, weren't you?" and then, he went to her grave. After he had performed his prayer, he prayed, "O God! May you fill this grave with light for the sake of my daily prayers."

He had a different affection towards the orphans

Due to the fact that our Prophet had a different affection towards the orphans, he would protect them and insist on their rights when they were acted unjustly towards. He would show concern for the orphans who were the children of martyr Companions and he did not leave them alone and he would fulfill what they needed. One day, a man poured out his troubles about the hardness of his heart and our Prophet advised him: "Do you want your heart to be softened and to gain what you need? Then, you should behave affectionately towards the orphans, caress their heads. Make them eat what you eat and so your heart will become soft and gain what you need."

He behaved towards women courteously

Our dear Prophet never discriminated between the women and the men. When they needed or wanted to learn something, he never rejected it and fulfilled what they needed and answered their questions. Particularly, he never broke old women's hearts and pleased them.

He had a different love towards children

Our Prophet had a different kind of love towards the children. He became very happy when he saw a child. He would take, hug, caress, and kiss him or her. He would greet every child he saw or came across and asked how he or she was. He talked to them in a friendly way and even behaved like a child with them. While he was with children, he talked to them according to their level of understanding and advised them. When he had a mount, he used to take the children to the place where they wanted to go. He was so close to the children that one day, he had a race with the children when he saw them.

Our affectionate Prophet could not put up with children crying and wanted them consoled. When he heard a child crying, he even made prayer shorter to enable the mother to deal with her child. Our Prophet said about it: "Whoever consoles his or her child crying, God will give the blessing as much as he or she will satisfy with."

He was merciful

Because of his creation our Prophet never behaved badly to those who did him harm and he forgave them and did not want to take revenge. He never rejected those who wanted to be saved and to be forgiven but for the wars. He accepted them to believe in God. When our Prophet entered the city for the conquest of Mecca with his crowded army, most of his enemies were helpless and wanted our Prophet to help them. Even then, when our Prophet was powerful enough to do whatever he wanted with them, he announced that he forgave his enemies. He even forgave Iqrima, son of Abu Jahil and Wahshi who killed Hamza, our Prophet's paternal uncle.

He would keep his word

Our dear Prophet could be considered the most cautious person in keeping his word. As he kept his word which he promised to his friends, he was faithful to the contract which he made with his enemies. Even before his Prophethood, he showed his loyalty to his word, to exemplify, he had waited for one of his friends for three days at the place they agreed to meet and he did not leave the place thinking his friend wouldn't come anymore.

He was the most courteous

Our dear Prophet was the most courteous, blameless, elegant, lovely, and sensitive of all people. He behaved towards everyone delicately and softly. When he was asked a question, he always answered it in a gentle and soft way. When one of his Companions or family called him, he always answered him or her very softly.

He used to listen intently to the one asking him about a matter and he did not leave him/her till he or she left him first. He never interrupted anyone. He greeted the one whom he came across first and he first began to shake hands until the man who he met took his hand away, and he never turned his face till the time that the man turned his face first. Also, he kneeled down when he sat with another man.

He had dignity

God's Messenger was dignified, serious, and excellent. When people saw him, they trembled in fear with his Prophetic dignity. However, after a while, people realized how affectionate he was. Our Prophet's every speech was full of wisdom. He never spoke useless words and never gossiped. Because he never broke anyone's heart, if he witnessed such a case he would undoubtedly warn that person.

He preferred to smile instead of laugh and when he smiled, his eyes lit up with joy. He never laughed loudly. When he liked something, he smiled as much as his teeth could be seen and his teeth shone like pearls. When he was walking, he never looked to the right or the left; he always looked ahead and walked with humble steps. His manner was silent and he spoke when required. Also, he warned people being prejudiced about a matter without knowing the essence and the facts of it.

He was always just

Our dear Prophet took justice into account in each decision and action and never discriminated people. He was very careful about justice. He did not want to harm anyone. He disapproved of tyranny and said all the time: "A Muslim is the brother of another Muslim and he/she never oppresses to him/her."

He attached importance to the young

Our dear Prophet generally chose the revelation clerks from the young and permitted them to give a legal pronouncement (*fatwa*). He appointed young teachers and made young commanders take charge of the armies consisting of many old Companions. He gave the flag to Zayd ibn Thabit in Tabuk and again he gave the flag to Ali ibn Abu Talib in Badr. He also listed the young who were faithful to God and worshipped God willingly among those who would be happy under the shade of the Divine Throne in the Day of Judgment.

GREETINGS TO YOU, OUR PROPHET

The essence of believing the unity of God and pure slavery is our prayer. The important thing in the prayer is to be aware of the fact that there is someone to answer all our prayers. The greatest means for the acceptance of a prayer is to bless our Prophet, that is, we want God to have mercy on our Prophet and give him the great position and extend his intercession circle to intercede before starting the prayer.

The greeting means to repeat and acknowledge him to be our master. That is, "O God! We believe in Muhammad and accept all the judgments, thoughts, amendments he brought." He fulfilled the duty of Prophethood perfectly."

OUR SINGLE HELPER DURING THE JUDGMENT DAY

When God gathers all the people in the Judgment Day, the sun will be very close to us, which means the gathering place (the area of resurrection) will be very hot. People will not be able to endure these trouble and agony, so they will seek a savior and say: "Please! Let's find an intercessor" and go to Prophet Adam to help them. However, Adam will send people to Noah; Noah will send them to Moses; Moses will send them to Jesus; and Jesus will send them to Muhammad, peace be upon them, saying that being the helper in this tremendous day has been bestowed upon the Prophet Muhammad, peace and blessings be upon him.

People will apply, in an inexplicable need, to the last Messenger of God and say:

"You are the last Messenger and the most loved by God. God forgave your past and future sins. Could you intercede for us? You see our positions."

Prophet Muhammad, peace and blessings be upon him, will come under the Divine Throne and prostrate in the presence of God, afterwards, God will inspire him the most excellent thanks and praise with the words which God did not teach to anyone before. The Prophet will implore God with every kind of praises. Afterwards, God will say: "Raise your head, O Muhammad! Speak, and your word will be listened. Wish, and your wish will be bestowed. Intercede, and your intercession will be fulfilled."

He will raise his head and will implore:

"O God! Grant my *ummah* to me! Save my *ummah*! Forgive my *ummah*!"

Then, God will say:

"O Muhammad! Go and take those, who have a bit of belief in their hearts the size of one grain," and the Prophet will do what is said.

People will be saved from the trouble by means of our Prophet's intercession on the Day of Judgment. If we want to reach his great help on that hard day we should always bless and take him as a model in our lives. May God accept us as those who are honored with our Prophet's intercession.

SINCERITY AND PATIENCE

FROM THE QUR'AN

O you who believe! Seek help (against all kinds of hardships and tribulations) through persevering patience and the Prayer; surely God is with the persevering and patient. (Al-Baqarah, 2:153).

Such are those upon whom are blessings from their Lord (such as forgiveness, answering their calls and satisfying their needs) and mercy (to come in the form of help in both this world and Hereafter, and favors in Paradise beyond human imagination); and they are the rightly guided ones. (Al-Baqarah, 2:157).

FROM THE LAST MESSENGER

The Hearts

Our Prophet said: "Certainly, God does not attach importance to your physical appearance or words but to your deeds and thoughts in your hearts."

The deeds of Muslims

Our dear Prophet said: "I am amazed at Muslims' deeds because their deeds are good completely and this is the only thing special to them. As they thank God when they experience a fine incident, they win. They are patient when they experience a saddening or harmful incident and they win again."

THOSE WHO LOVE EACH OTHER FOR ALLAH'S ACCEPTANCE

Abu Hurayra told about a case that our Prophet mentioned: "A man set out to visit one of his friends living in another place. God sent an angel and assigned him to observe the man on the road."

When the man met the angel, the angel asked him: "Where are you going?"

The man said: "I am going to visit my religious brother."

The angel asked again: "Do you have any business with him?"

The man replied: "No, there is nothing like that. I love him for the sake of God's acceptance."

Therefore the angel said: "I am an envoy that was entrusted with informing you that God loves you as you love your brother for the sake of God's acceptance."

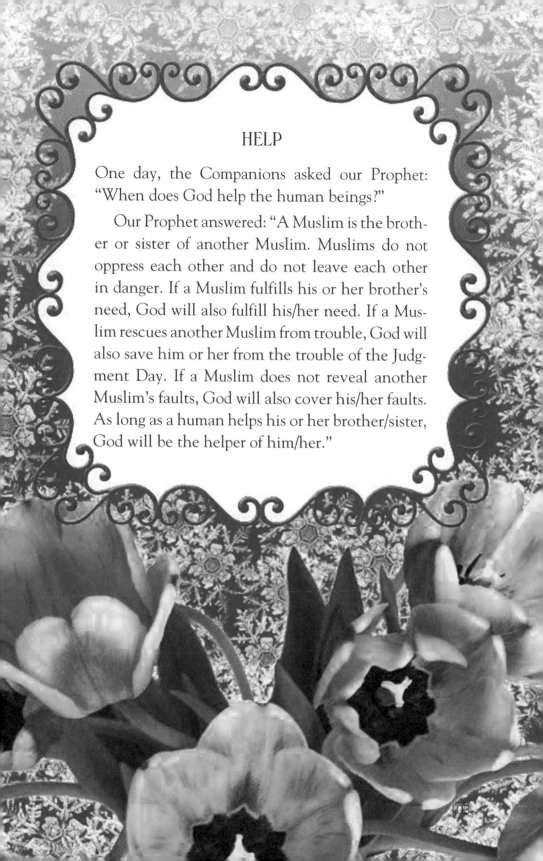

HELP

One day, the Companions asked our Prophet: "When does God help the human beings?"

Our Prophet answered: "A Muslim is the brother or sister of another Muslim. Muslims do not oppress each other and do not leave each other in danger. If a Muslim fulfills his or her brother's need, God will also fulfill his/her need. If a Muslim rescues another Muslim from trouble, God will also save him or her from the trouble of the Judgment Day. If a Muslim does not reveal another Muslim's faults, God will also cover his/her faults. As long as a human helps his or her brother/sister, God will be the helper of him/her."

THE ANGEL WAS ANSWERING

When our dear Prophet was sitting with his Companions, a man insulted Abu Bakr and made him sad. However, Abu Bakr remained silent, that man did the same thing again. Abu Bakr said nothing again. After the man made him sad three times, Abu Bakr answered to him. After a while, the last Messenger of God left Abu Bakr and walked away. Abu Bakr asked: "Did you get angry at me?"

Our Prophet answered: "No! An angel descended from the heavens and was declaring the insulting words untrue. As you remained silent, that angel answered instead of you. When you took revenge by answering him, that angel went and the Satan sat. When the Satan sits in a place, I cannot stay there."

A SEED IN MY PALM

I am not from here. I came here from distant places from the other end of the world by crossing extensive deserts and plenty of lakes. I took a seed and came here.

I hope the delivery address is here. I should stop now. I gave all my goods but for this seed. Do not ask the reason. All I know is my arrival by bringing the universe along with me, putting the stars into my pocket and the rains into my eyes. When I looked at my palm, I saw my citizen and then Asia and I heard the prayer of Yasawi, Taptuk and Sarı Saltuk. Then, I saw Anatolia and Jerusalem and the children had kites. I saw Palestine and the hope. I came here with a dove and a city in my palm.

This world will have grandchildren and they will set up cities like Mecca, Baghdad, Beirut, and Venice. They will spread hope around. When I was coming here, I thought many things to be told and I came here to call everyone to "good" and I hope that the gardeners watering trees will encircle throughout the country and environmentalists will become a thing of the past. The people will wander around and a little girl will give a daisy to her mother.

Not only Istanbul but also everywhere, everyone will realize the tulips in the hearts. Firstly, the city inside of us will

change and then Istanbul will change. The cities where people live are the products of the settlers in them.

The land dried and it is high time that we should water it before we see nightmares among the long buildings, let's give a place to trees and palms.

An envoy cannot be blamed for his mission. If I brought a bunch of roses, open your hands and hearts. If I came with a city, a human and a tree in my palm, open your palms. Let's turn seeds into trees. It is time to go on the way and give a place in your land; there is a seed in my palm.

BELIEF IN THE HEREAFTER

FROM THE QUR'AN

It never occurs that a soul dies save by God's leave, at a time appointed. So whoever desires the reward of this world, We give him of it (in the world); and whoever desires the reward of the Hereafter, We give him of it; and We will soon reward the thankful. (Al-Imran, 3:145).

Assuredly you have in God's Messenger an excellent example to follow for whoever looks forward to God and the Last Day, and remembers and mentions God much. (Al-Ahzab, 33:21).

All praise and gratitude are for God to Whom belongs whatever is in the heavens and whatever is on the earth (for it is He Who has created them and sustains them); and for Him are all praise and gratitude in the Hereafter (as it is He alone Who will found it as an eternal abode for His servants). He is the All-Wise, the All-Aware. (As-Saba, 34:1).

FROM THE LAST MESSENGER

People will wake up

Our Prophet said: "Be like a passenger or a guest in the world! People are sleeping and when they die, they will wake up."

The account of five things

Our Prophet said that a human will not be able to leave before he or she gives account of five things. They are; where people spent their lives, what kinds of deeds they did in the world, where they earned items and where they spent them, where they spent their youth and to what extend they practiced what they knew.

Three things will follow us

Our Prophet said: "When a person dies, three things will follow him/her: The goods, family, and the deeds. The goods and family come back from the grave. The one which will stay with him or her is the deeds."

THERE IS NOTHING WHICH YOU WILL TAKE FROM ME

The last Messenger of God said: "Three people will be in-terrogated in the Judgment Day. The first of them is the one who died during the war and he will be brought in the presence of God and He will make known to him His favors and he will recognize them. Then, God will ask: 'What did you do in such blessings?'

That human will answer: 'I fought as much as I became a martyr.'

God will say: 'You are lying; you fought in order to make people believe that you are a brave man and they said so.'

The second is the one who learned a branch of knowledge or science and taught it to other people and read the Qur'an and he is brought in the presence of God and He will make known to him His favors and he will recognize them. Then, God asks: 'What did you do in such blessings?'

That human will answer: 'I learned knowledge and taught it to the others and read the Qur'an.'

God says: 'You are lying; you learned it so that people would call you a "scholar." You read the Qur'an so that people would say to you "the one who reads the Qur'an well" and they said so.'

The third is the one who God bestowed prosperity and every kind of items and this man is brought in the presence of God and He will make known to him His favors and he will recognize them. Then, God asks: 'What did you do in such blessings?'

That man will answer: 'I delivered them wherever you wanted me to give.'

God says: 'You are lying. You did them so that people will say to you "how generous he is" and they said so.'"

TRUE BASHFULNESS

Ibn Masud narrates: "One day, our dear Prophet said: 'Be a bashful.'

We said: 'Thanks be to God! We are bashful enough.'

However the Prophet said: 'Be bashful as much as possible. Those who are bashful enough should take control of his or her thoughts and mind and the stomach and the things in his or her stomach. Do not forget the death and decomposition. If you want to gain the Hereafter, you should leave the temporary beauties of the world. Namely, if a person behaves so, that will be bashful enough towards God.'"

THE DAY WHEN THE *SUR* IS BLOWN

After verses 8 and 9 of *surah* Al-Muddathir were revealed, the Messenger said: "While Israfil waits to blow the *Sur*, how will I enjoy life?" One of the Companions said: "What do you advise us to say?"

Our Prophet said: "God is sufficient for us; how excellent a Guardian He is! We trust and rely on God."

THE EIGHT GATES OF PARADISE

Our Prophet said:

"The first gate of Paradise is the one on which "There is no deity but Allah" were written, belonging to Prophets, martyrs, and the generous. The second gate belongs to those who performed ablution and prayer completely; the third one belongs to those giving the one fortieth of their incomes distributed as alms. The fourth gate belongs to those who advise kindness and make people avoid malicious actions. The fifth one belongs to those taking control of their worldly desires and those who fasted. The sixth belongs to those who performed pilgrimage to Mecca; the seventh gate is the gate of the fighters for the Islamic faith. The eighth is the gate of those having God-fearing behavior and not looking at those forbidden by the religion."

If a Muslim gives some asset (such as money, time, knowledge) which he/she has for the sake of God, each doorkeeper of Paradise will welcome and invite him/her enter there.

THE QUESTION OF MUNKAR AND NAKIR

One day, after our Prophet buried a dead person, he said: "Wish the forgiveness of God for your brother and wish God to make his belief constant. He is definitely being interrogated."

And he told the question of the angels called Munkar and Nakir that will interrogate the man in the grave: "Those two angels will ask the man who his Lord is."

And that man says: "My Lord is God"

The angels ask: "What is your religion?"

That man answers: "My religion is Islam"

The angels ask: "Who was sent to you?"

That human replies: "Muhammad, the Prophet of God"

The angels ask: "What is your deed?"

That human answers: "I read and believed in the Qur'an. And I also approved of it."

IN THE DAY OF JUDGMENT

Our Prophet said: "God will address the people in this way: "O human being! I was ill but you did not visit me!"

That human will ask: "O God, how could I have visited you? You are the Lord of the worlds! You are free from illnesses."

God will say: "O human being! Don't you know that one of my people got sick but you didn't visit him. If you had visited him, you would have gained my contentment."

God will say to some people: "O human being! I wanted food from you but you did not feed me."

That human being will ask: "My Lord! How could I have fed you? You are the Lord of the worlds; you are free from hunger and you do not need to eat or drink."

God will address that human: "One of my people was hungry. He wanted food from you but you did not give it. If you had given the food you would have gained my love, acceptance, and contentment."

God will also address some people: "O human being! I wanted water from you and you did not give it."

That human will ask: "My Lord! You are the Lord of the worlds. You do not need anything to drink."

God will say: "O human being! One of my people was thirsty but you did not give it. If you had given water to him you would have gained my acceptance and contentment."

IF ONLY

Our dear Prophet said: "When the permanent people of Hell and Muslims come together, the unbelievers will ask the Muslims: 'Aren't you Muslims?'

Muslims will say: 'Yes'

The unbelievers: 'Then, is not being a Muslim enough to be saved from the Fire? And you came to Hell with us.'

The Muslims: 'We have some sins and we are here to suffer for our sins.'

God hears this conversation and commands that the Muslims should be taken from Hell and when the unbelievers see it, they will say 'If only we were Muslims and were rescued from Hell!'"

After our Prophet told it he read the verse:

> Alif. Lam. Ra. These are the Revelations of the Book, a Qur'an clear in itself and clearly showing the truth. Again and again will those who disbelieve wish that they had been Muslims. (Al-Hijr, 15:1–2).

THEY WILL BE KEPT FOR THE HEREAFTER

Abu Bakr and our Prophet had lunch when verses 7 and 8 of *surah* Zilzal were sent. Abu Bakr stood up and asked: "My dear Prophet! Will we take the equivalent of all our bad deeds in the Hereafter?"

Our Prophet said: "All the upsetting events you had are the equivalent of your bad deeds and the equivalent of your good deeds will be kept for the Hereafter."

WHEN THE *SUR* IS BLOWED

Our dear Prophet explained about Israfil and the Doomsday: "Israfil, one of the great four angels, will blow on a trumpet called the *Sur* which only God knows its true nature and the end of the world will occur. Because of God's mercy on the believers, the souls of them will be taken at first, and the unbelievers will suffer the Doomsday."

God says: "When the *Sur* is blown, all the creatures will die, and then when the *Sur* is blown once again, they will stand up and look at each other."

TWO GRAVES

Our dear Prophet saw two graves and said: "These two people suffer torment for a sin which people neglect. One of them suffers anguish because he did not clean himself up after urination and the other suffers anguish because he destroyed the friendship among people by gossiping."

Then, our Prophet divided a fresh green branch into two parts and planted each of them on both graves and people around him asked: "Why did you do that?"

Our Prophet said: "I hope that their torment will be reduced as long as they are green. I hope that they will wish mercy on these people."

THE GATE OF PARADISE

Our Prophet said: "I will want the gate of Paradise to be opened in the Day of Judgment." The angel called Hazin at the door says: "Who are you?"

I will answer: "I am Muhammad"

The angel says: "I will open it for you. I was ordered not to open it to anyone except for you."

THE LIFE ADVENTURE OF A HUMAN BEING

Ibrahim Haqqi of Erzurum (1703–1780), a prolific, encyclopedic Sufi guide and writer, summarizes the life journey of man as follows:

"A human being has four different worlds: the uterus, the world, the place where the souls of the dead await the Day of Judgment and the Hereafter. As a child does not want to be born, the human does not want to leave the world. As long as a child finds pleasure in his mother's milk, he does not want to return to his previous place and when the people reunite with God, they do not want to return to the world and forget it."

IBRAHIM IBN ADHAM'S MONEY FOR TURKISH BATHING

One day, Ibrahim ibn Adham, one of the important saints, wanted to go into the Turkish bath and said to the keeper of the bath: "I have no money, could you let me go into the bath?"

The keeper of the bath said: "No entrance without money."

Ibrahim ibn Adham insisted but the keeper of the bath did not allow him to go into it. After that he left there and

then he cried loudly. The people hearing this voice, said to Ibrahim ibn Adham : "You do not need to cry so much. We shall give you the money."

Then Ibrahim ibn Adham told the people: "Do you think that I am crying because I could not go into the bath? I am not crying because of this. People do not let me go into the bath without money in the world. What if, just like this, I will be rejected in the Hereafter as those who do not deserve Paradise and will not be accepted there?"

ETERNAL BEAUTY REQUIRES AN ENDLESS WORLD

Let's listen to the singing of the birds and splashing of water in spring. Let's watch the beauty of emerald-green trees and all the plants; let's look at the rise and the setting of the sun and moonlight on a clear night. Let's imagine all the beauty in the universe.

This kind of pretty sceneries is a manifestation of God's beauty. God shows us God's own beauty with these successive sceneries. We admire this beauty and God wants to make us know Himself and we try to know Him.

If God prevents us to see the beauty, the blessing will turn into a torment, the affection will turn into a calamity, and the mind will turn into a device which gives us anguish. However, God is free from this kind of unpleasant behavior. What makes the blessing a favor and makes the mind to be proper enough to enjoy life is the continuity of those blessings. God will set apart a place, where He will show His Divine beauty continuously, and He will assemble us for judgment there.

Moreover, His beauty is eternal; therefore a world is required for the beauty to continue. As we admire the beauty of His manifestations, we will admire at the beauty when we watch it one day, *"Looking up toward their Lord."* (Al-Qiyamah, 75:23)

THE GUIDING LIGHTS

❀ When asking from God, ask for Him.

❀ The things which are not bound to their real owner are ownerless.

❀ One who does not care for his Hereafter has a risky end.

❀ The duty of a hero of belief, who is aware of his servanthood, is to be "zero" before the Infinite.

❀ Those who cannot nullify themselves can never unite with the Infinite.

❀ Those who pass over the Bridge of Sirat easily are the people living on the Straight Path.

❀ The real heroism of compassion is having no expectation, including Paradise.

❀ Paradise is a manifestation of the love of God.

❀ The deadliest virus is to consider one's self well and sufficient.

❀ Heedless people show their deficit of belief in the Hereafter, for belief in the Hereafter necessitates seriousness.

❀ The gain and loss at the end of the test of this world is so huge that people who are subject of such an end cannot live heedlessly.

❀ To correct the faults of the past is impossible; however it is possible not to make the same faults with the help of God, with a sincere repentance.

❀ The suffering of a believer about the guidance of others is in proportion to his belief in God and the Hereafter. The more belief he has the more suffering he has experienced.

✿ To revenge with Hell is a monstrous feeling. It is the way of a believer to say "No my Lord, I cannot approve one's being in the Fire eternally, even if it's my enemy who behaved badly to me."

✿ One of the causes contaminating the mind is to be busy with the attitudes and behaviors of others.

✿ Touchiness and envy may cause more harm than the enemies do.

✿ Petty people deal with petty things.

✿ The future is not entrusted to the one whose future is not bright.

✿ Backbiting and gossip are deadly viruses for a community.

✿ We should always take care to behave according to our own values in order to make our words effective.

✿ To be a perfect believer, one should be undisturbed upon hearing his faults.

✿ Changing one's character in one aspect brings the possibility of changing in any aspect.

✿ The most unfortunate ones are those who do not care about their end, and who pass away suddenly, with lots of deficits.

✿ To reach our essence means to revive with our own values once again.

BACKBITING AND SINFUL SUSPICION

FROM THE QUR'AN

Remember and mention your Lord within yourself (in the depths of your heart), most humbly and in awe, not loud of voice, at morning and evening. And do not be among the neglectful. (Al-A'raf, 7:205).

A kind word and forgiving (people's faults) are better than almsgiving followed by taunting. God is All-Wealthy and Self-Sufficient, (absolutely independent of the charity of people), All-Clement (Who shows no haste in punishing.) (Al-Baqarah, 2:263).

And say to My servants that they should always speak (even when disputing with others) that which is the best. Satan is ever ready to sow discord among them. For Satan indeed is a manifest enemy for humankind. (Al-Isra, 17:53).

FROM THE LAST MESSENGER

The last Prophet said: "God protects from Hell in the Hereafter the one who protects a Muslim from a mischief maker. And whoever slanders an innocent Muslim, God imprisons him or her to Hell until he or she is cleaned from his or her sins."

GOSSIP

When Junaidi Baghdadi, an Islamic scholar, was in a mosque one day, someone approached him and asked for some donation to buy some food. Junaidi Baghdadi gave the person an appraising glance and thought he was healthy enough to work and wondered why he was begging.

At night, when Junaidi Baghdadi slept, he had a dream, and in his dream someone brought him some meat to eat. He asked what kind of meat it was as it smelt very bad. The person said it was the meat of the beggar he saw today.

The person who brought the meat said: "Eat this meat Junaidi Baghdadi!"

He answered: "How can I eat this, it smells awful and it is the flesh of a man."

The person said: "You ate this in the mosque today, so you can eat again."

Then Junaidi Baghdadi understood that he had gossiped about the beggar. He got up and prayed. He left the house immediately in order to look for the beggar and he found him near a river. The beggar looked at Junaidi Baghdadi and said "You gossiped about me. Do you regret your action?"

Junaidi Baghdadi said: "Yes, deeply!"

The beggar uttered the verse: *(The Pharaoh) said to those around him: "Do you not hear (what he is saying)?"* (Ash-Shu'ara, 26:25)

HE DOES NOT KNOW WHAT THE LIE IS…

Mehmet Akif Ersoy, the poet of the Turkish national anthem, was an honest man. No one heard him tell a single lie during his lifetime. Moreover, he would get very angry with those who told lies. He was very careful about his words.

One of his friends asked "Is it true" when he said something. He got furious and said "Never ask me again if I am telling the truth."

The education of that time taught him even the joke of a lie was unacceptable in our belief.

GOLDEN GENERATION

This year, as usual, conferences, meetings, seminars, and lessons have followed each other. I definitely know that I shouldn't get tired. Whenever my fatigue falls in my mind, I always think about the result. When I fall into the darkness of the misery, I think of my ideals, my students, and their bright futures. I have been granted the opportunity to teach the golden generation. This is enough to be worth being happy.

There were a few minutes for the class to start and I realized Selma while I was mooning in the corridor. She asked me if I had free time to talk. She desperately wanted to talk to me. I was anxious because a lot of things fell into my mind as to whether it was an undesirable thing that she wanted to speak to me about. Was it about the school, or her family or something else? Up to that time she always seemed to be very reluctant to share her problems with the others. I took her and we sat in the teacher's room.

Selma started to speak:

"We went to Ms. Derya with my friend Zeynep after the social sciences exam. Ms. Derya told us a story of one of her teachers which touched me a lot and which reminded me of you. In her story there was a teacher called Aziz.

Aziz was a very self sacrificing teacher who devoted his life for his students. Though he could have easily found a very well-paid job in his own country, he denied all these opportunities and left his country just to teach the students who are in need of a good education.

He generally passed his time outside his home dealing with the problems of his students. When he was at home he did his best to educate his own children.

However, one day one of his children said something which hurt Aziz deeply. One of his child said: "I am not happy with you father because you don't give me much time. You are always out."

Aziz got very distressed. He shared this with one of his best friends, Sedat. Aziz said to Sedat: "My dear brother, you have witnessed that when I was outside I was always interested in the problems of my students. I never lost time for nothing and when I found time, I always allotted it to my family. You know this and I want you to be my witness in the Hereafter." Sedat's eyes filled with tears and he said: "Yes my brother, undoubtedly I bear witness to your sacrificing."

Selma was crying while telling these. And some words came out of her mouth. She said: "When I was listening to the story of Aziz, you came into my mind. O my dear teacher, you are the same as Aziz. You left your family, your home, everything you have, and you came here to teach me. But I witness that you gave all your time for us. I certainly appreciate your self-determinism and self-sacrificing."

Meanwhile, I swallowed my tears and thanked God quietly.

BELIEF IN DIVINE DESTINY

FROM THE QUR'AN

Surely, We have created each and every thing by (precise) measure. (Al-Qamar, 54:49).

Say: "Nothing befalls us except what God has decreed for us; He is our Guardian and Owner; and in God let the believers put all their trust." (At-Tawbah, 9:51).

No affliction befalls except by God's leave. Whoever believes in God (truly and sincerely), He guides his heart (to true knowledge of His eternal Will, and how He acts with regard to the life of His creatures, and so leads him to humble submission to Him, and to peace and serenity). God has full knowledge of all things. (At-Taghabun, 64:11).

Every soul (person) is bound to taste death, and We try you through the bad and the good things (of life) by way of testing (so that your real character and rank may reveal itself). In fact, you are on the way to return to Us (to finally be brought to Our Presence). (Al-Anbiya, 21:35).

With Him are the keys to the Unseen; none knows them but He. And He knows whatever is on land and in the sea; and not a leaf falls but He knows it; and neither is there a grain in the dark layers of earth, nor anything green or dry, but is (recorded) in a Manifest Book. (Al-An'am, 6:59).

FROM THE LAST PROPHET

Without believing....

The last Messenger of God said: "A person cannot be a true believer without accepting undoubtedly that goodness or badness does not befall us without the permission of God. It is only with the permission of God that people can overcome the problems they face."

Consenting with the fate

The last Messenger said: "One of the ways for people's happiness is to consent to destiny, which is known absolutely by God."

If...

The last Messenger said: "Struggle for good things and beg God for help. If something bad befalls you, never say 'If I had done it in a different way, it would not have happened to me,' because the word 'if' opens a gateway to Satan."

Dreams

Our Prophet said about dreams: "*Hulm*, a depressing dream, comes from Satan. If one of you dreams it, he or she should avoid explaining it to anyone. He or she should also take shelter in his or her belief, trusting God. If he or she does so, Satan cannot be harmful for him or her.

If you have a lovely dream, you can only mention about it to your loved ones. If you ask for is interpretation to your loved one, you should never ask another one. You shouldn't ruin your good fate."

JUSTICE OF ALLAH

The Messenger said: "While Prophet Moses was delivering a religious instruction one day, one of the audiences asked him who the most knowledgeable scholar in the world was.

The Prophet Moses said 'me' and upon this God said: 'I have a human being in the middle of two seas who is more knowledgeable than you.'

The Prophet Moses asked: 'O my Lord, how can I find him?'

God said: 'Take a fish and put it in a bag then set off. Whenever the fish goes out of the bag and disappears, then it is the place you will be able to find him.'

Moses did so and set off with a boy named Yusha ibn Nun. When they arrived at a huge rock, they both fell asleep in the shadow of the rock. The fish left the bag and dived into the water making its way through a hole.

They both followed the fish and they found a man sleeping, wrapping himself in his own clothes.

The man was Khidr, who is sent by God for those who are in need of help. The Prophet Moses greeted him and said that he wanted to be friends.

Khidr said: 'O Moses, you are not as strong to become my friend. I have some knowledge given by God but you are not aware of this. You have some knowledge that I don't know, as well.'

The Prophet Moses said: 'You will find me as a patient man and I won't disobey your rules.'

Khidr said: 'If you are determined to follow, you should never ask anything till I ask you first.'

They set off together in order to get on a ship. People aboard recognized Khidr so they did not ask for the fee. Upon their embarking, Khidr made a hole on the ground of the ship using an ax.

After witnessing this incident, the Prophet Moses said:

'They took us to their ship for free but you made a hole in it! Do you want to kill them? This is not a good thing.'

Khidr answered:

'Didn't I tell you, you could never be patient with me.'

The Prophet Moses said: 'Sorry, I absolutely forgot about it. Please, continue our friendship.'

After a while, they left the ship and started to walk on the seaside. Khidr saw a young boy playing on the sand. He killed the boy suddenly which shocked Prophet Moses.

The Prophet Moses said: 'You killed the young boy without a reason. How can you do this? You committed a very big sin.'

Khidr answered: 'Didn't I tell you, you could never be patient with me.'

The Prophet Moses said: 'If I raise an objection against your doings from now on, you may end our friendship because you accepted my excuse twice.'

They carried on their journey. They arrived in a town and asked for food from its natives. The natives were reluctant to give food. Meanwhile, they saw a wall turning into a ruin. Khidr held the wall and repaired it.

The Prophet Moses couldn't stand again and said: 'Though the natives were reluctant to give us some food, you helped them.'

Upon this, Khidr said: 'Your last words have meant we need to part ways. So, I will make all these three incidents clear for you.'

He continued: 'In our first incident, the ship belonged to some poor people working in the sea. I tried to make a defect on their ship because on their way there was a cruel king who seizes all powerful and flawless ships. So I chose the lesser of two evils and I helped them in this way.

Secondly, the boy that I killed, in spite of his innocent appearance, was going to be a very cruel man in the future for both his parents and society. By killing him I saved them and also I saved the boy from going to Hell.

Lastly, the wall belonged to two orphan boys and under it was a big treasure. If the wall had pulled down, the natives would have taken the treasure since its owners were still children. Repairing the wall, I helped them keep the treasure when they became adults.'"

This story was mentioned in the Qur'an. All the stories in the Qur'an give us some lessons about our lives. We can infer from the story that without knowing the real and maybe hidden reason of something, we should not comment on it.

THE DESTINY OF EVERYTHING
UNTIL THE END OF THE WORLD

Ubadah ibn as-Samit, may God be pleased with him, gathered his children nearing his death and said: "My dear children, as God knows everything from pre-eternity, He makes His angels write all the things which occur in the universe. Everybody has a destiny which is written in this way and in which one has to believe without any doubt. If you become suspicious about this reality you will never be able to become a true believer."

A Muslim should strongly believe that God knows everything but this doesn't mean He forces us to do the things that He knows. He determines our destiny according to our inclinations, doings, and actions. He left us free to draw our way but that doesn't mean that he doesn't know what we incline. He is All-Knowing: He knows the past, the present, and the future. *"Is it conceivable that One Who creates should not know?"* (Al-Mulk, 67:14).

WHAT IS WHAT IN BELIEVING DESTINY?

God has the absolute knowledge of everything. *"He is the All-Subtle (penetrating to the most minute dimensions of all things), the All-Aware."* (Al-Mulk, 67:14).

An example of belief in destiny is as follows: Imagine you are planning to eat some well-cooked meat at night. You go to a butcher to buy some meat and you eat it at dinner. As God knows all your actions from pre-eternity (beyond time and space), He knows that you would buy some meat and eat it. If He approves your action, He gives you the permission of doing whatever you plan.

God's knowledge includes everything that happened and that will happen. The fact that God knows everything pre-eternally does not make a person free from the responsibilities of the actions he did using his own power of will. *"Divine Destiny is a kind of knowledge, and knowledge is dependent on the thing known. In other words, conceptual knowledge is not fundamental to determining the external existence of what is known. In its external existence, the known depends upon the Divine Power acting through the Divine Will."* (Nursi, The Words, p. 482).

LANGUAGE OF VIBRATION

One of the special characteristics bestowed to the animals is being aware of their surroundings. Thus, they can communicate with each other. By doing so each animal uses a language special to its own species. Some animal species use special scents while some others make sounds to communicate with each other.

Termites send messages to their friends by shaking their bodies. These animals can also make connections by scents like their friend ants to which they are similar in appearance. They are famous for building their homes in layers even though they cannot see. Their houses, in which they put all the essential materials they will need, can reach 7 meters in height. They build their houses on soil or on trees and they are fed on barks.

While they contribute to nature by building their houses on trees, this could dangerous for themselves because some trees are damp and hot especially when they begin to decay, and on them live many fungus and bacteria being the cause of disease for termites.

What do the termites on trees do for this danger? In fact, the ants, friends of termites, produce disinfectants to protect themselves.

When one of the termites is infected with bacteria, it starts shaking its body. This vibration is a visible message for the others not to come to the area. The infected termite generally dies but it won't leave the area until it makes it clear that the area is diseased, and he waits up until his death. The others are protected in this way. Basically, the diseased termite, even in the last moments of his life, doesn't leave its duty to make others live, and for the future of its colony, it sacrifices itself.

THE GUIDING LIGHTS

❖ Whoever crushes an ant intentionally should be afraid of an evil befalling him or her.

❖ The way of not criticizing destiny is to question yourself unprejudicedly.

❖ A true believer may consent to the events which took place and completed but he or she shouldn't consent to the occurring of the future because we look to the past through the window of destiny but we look to the future in terms of the power of will.

❖ It is good for your personal life to be patient for the difficulties, however, leaving the others with their hardness and sufferings is a cruelty.

❖ God's examination of us is just to show us Himself. He already knows everything but we don't, so we need to know Him.

❖ Not to comply with the causes is a sort of disrespectfulness towards God.

❖ Trusting your good deeds for the Hereafter diminishes one's trust in God.

❖ May God always help us, because without His help we cannot realize anything. Nothing happens without His permission.

❖ Being right does not necessitate becoming rude.

❖ Not sharing the problems of his or her brothers in belief is a deep gap in one's belief.

- Tears are the composition of the feelings of one's heart.

- A true believer must himself or herself avoid committing sins before he or she advises others to stay away from them. In this way, they will be effectual in their words to others.

- One cannot commit a certain sin just for a possible good deed.

- A true believer's love to his or her Messenger can only be realistic by just aiming to spread His name to all humanity.

- Books may only be worthwhile as long as they take you to God, otherwise; they can be counted as meaningless.

- The one who has conceit and arrogance in his or her heart cannot find the true belief of God as well as His love.

HUMILITY, TOLERANCE AND POLITENESS

FROM THE QUR'AN

The (true) servants of the All-Merciful are they who move on the earth gently and humbly, and when the ignorant, foolish ones address them (with insolence or vulgarity, as befits their ignorance and foolishness), they respond with (words of) peace (without engaging in hostility with them) (Al-Furqan, 25:63).

Let not those among you who are favored with resources swear that they will no longer give to the kindred, the needy, and those who have emigrated in God's cause (even though those wealthy ones suffer harm at the hands of the latter). Rather, let them pardon and forbear. Do you not wish that God should forgive you? God is All-Forgiving, All-Compassionate. (An-Nur, 24:22).

Only they (truly) believe in Our signs and Revelations who, when they are mentioned of them (by way of advice and instruction), fall down in prostration, and glorify their Lord with His praise, and they do not behave with haughtiness. (As-Sajdah, 32:15).

FROM THE LAST MESSENGER

The Messenger of God said: "Three (kinds of people) will neither be spoken to by Allah on the Day of Resurrection, nor looked at, nor purified (from their sins), and shall receive a painful torment." He repeated that thrice, so Abu Dharr said, "They are failures and losers. Who are they, Messenger of Allah?" The Prophet replied, "The one dragging his lower garment, the one who is used to reminding people of his generosity towards them, and the one who sells his goods through false swearing."

A MOMENT

It was very common to gather in mosques to be informed by the Caliph Umar during his administration of the Islamic public. Mosques were the places in which people discussed and solved many problems.

The mosque was full of people on one of the days that the Caliph would make a speech. The Caliph Umar was a very punctual person and he disliked wasting time in vain.

While he was making his speech, he stopped for a moment and said something out of the topic:

"You were just a shepherd herding your father's camels."

People were all confused. They were lost as to what to say or do. However, they all waited for the speech to finish.

After the Caliph ended his speech, some people approached him and asked out of curiosity:

"We didn't clearly understand the sentence you uttered during your speech."

The Caliph, though being the administrator of a huge land, uttered these words modestly:

"During my speech, the thought of being a Caliph stroke me suddenly. I did not feel arrogantly proud but I was afraid to feel so. Hence, I reminded myself the past days of mine."

LET THE AFTERLIFE BE OURS...

Umar visited the Prophet one day to consult some important issues with him. In the Messenger's room was a bag full of some grains and processed leather. There was also a small straw mat on which the Messenger was resting and which left its trace on his face.

This touched Umar and he couldn't stop his tears from falling. Before his acceptance of Islam, he had never cried for anything. With Islam, as most people do, he became a very sensitive person.

When the Messenger asked why he was crying, he said: "O my dear Prophet, you are sitting on a mat whereas the other kings are all resting on very comfortable beds."

Upon this answer, the Prophet said: "O Umar, don't you want the Hereafter to be ours and this world be theirs?"

WHO IS THAT MAN?

Mehmet Akif Ersoy, the great poet of the Turkish national anthem, was known for his honesty and modesty. Reşat Nuri Güntekin, another famous author, witnessed this fact one day.

Güntekin was an undergraduate student. When he was waiting in his class for the lesson to start one day, someone, wearing ordinary and seemingly very cheap clothes, opened the door and came into the class. Güntekin did not know the man but he thought of him as a student. A strange thing happened for him because this unknown man sat on the lecturer's desk, not the student's.

Güntekin was surprised when he learned the man was a professor.

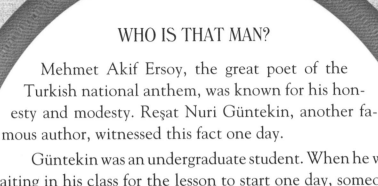

WORSHIP

FROM THE QUR'AN

You alone do We worship, and from You alone do we seek help. (Al-Fatiha, 1:5).

Surely, God is my Lord and your Lord, so worship Him. This is a straight path (to follow). (Al-Imran, 3:51).

Those who return in repentance to God, and those who worship God, and those who praise God, and those who travel (with such aims as conveying God's Message, or studying and making investigations for God's sake or reflecting on God's signs), and those who bow down in awe of God, and those who prostrate themselves before God in submission, and those who enjoin and promote what is right and good, and forbid and try to prevent evil, and those who keep to the bounds set by God: give glad tidings to the believers. (At-Tawbah, 9:112).

To Him belongs whoever is in the heavens and the earth. And those (the angels) who are with Him, never disdain to worship Him, nor do they ever weary. (Al-Anbiya, 21:19).

O you who believe! Bow down and prostrate yourselves (thus performing the Prayer), and fulfill all your other duties of worship to your Lord, and do (all the other commands of your Religion, which are all) good, so that you may prosper. (Al-Hajj, 22:77).

FROM THE LAST MESSENGER

Five Orders

The last Messenger of God said: "God ordered the Prophet Yahya to warn his tribe with five orders. Upon this, the Prophet Yahya gathered his tribe to inform them about the orders. The *masjid*, a small mosque, was filled with people. Then, the Prophet Yahya went through his speech.

He explained: 'God ordered me to perform five orders and also teach them to you. The first is to worship only God by not attributing any partners to him. The second is to pray regularly. By the way, while praying, looking around is a big shame. God only accepts the prayers which are performed sincerely. The third one is to fast. Fasting is such an invaluable worship that the smell of the mouth of a fasting performer is better than the musk (a beautiful scent) for God. The fourth is giving alms, that is, helping the poor or the ones in need. The fifth one is to think about the creation and the Creator. To illustrate this, just imagine a man who is running away from bandits and eventually find a sheltered place in which he can keep himself in secure. A person can only protect himself or herself from the Satan by deeply meditating God and His creation.'"

After telling the story, the last Messenger continued: "I order you five rules which were ordered to me by God. You should accept all the prohibitions and orders of God. You should also obey your administrators. You should spend your time and wealth to that way of God.

You shouldn't leave your Muslim friends, community. And, when necessary, you should migrate for your religion's sake. If you leave your Muslim community, it is tantamount to leaving your religion. Any revolt deriving from your displeasure of the community you are living with is not accepted in Islam and it is just an act of pre-Islamic Period of Ignorance."

WORSHIP

Worship is the expression of being a human and a slave of God. It is being thankful to God for all the blessings He bestowed to us. Being away from worship means being ungrateful towards God. Worship is a kind of meeting with God. If someone is away from worship, it is tantamount to be away from God. Worship is a sort of device which turns its lovers into angel-like beings. Unlike this fact, being away from worship may turn people into Satan-like attitudes. The best of worships is to love God and be beneficial for people.

ABLUTION AND THE DAILY PRAYERS

FROM THE QUR'AN

Those who believe in the Unseen; establish the Prayer in conformity with its conditions, and out of what We have provided for them (of wealth, knowledge, power, etc.,) they spend (to provide sustenance for the needy and in God's cause, purely for the good pleasure of God and without placing others under obligation). (Al-Baqarah 2:3).

(Let your concern be to) establish the Prayer in conformity with its conditions and pay the Prescribed Purifying Alms. Whatever good you send ahead (to your future life in this world and the next) to your own souls' account, you will find it with God. Whatever (good or evil) you do, surely God sees it well. (Al-Baqarah 2:110).

Those who believe and do good, righteous deeds, and establish the Prayer in conformity with its conditions, and pay the Prescribed Purifying Alms, their reward is with their Lord, and they will have no fear, nor will they grieve. (Al-Baqarah 2:277).

O you who believe! When the call is made for the Prayer on Friday, then move promptly to the remembrance of God (by listening to the sermon and doing the Prayer), and leave off business (and whatever else you may be preoccupied with). This is better for you, if you but knew. (Al-Jumu'ah 62:9).

FROM THE LAST MESSENGER

Being Clean

The last Messenger of God said: "If a person clears his body and does his ablution and afterwards wears very clean clothes before he falls asleep, an angel prays for him till the morning uttering these words: 'May God forgive you since you slept very clean.'"

Each prayer time

Our dear Prophet said: "Whenever a prayer time comes an angel says: 'O humans, get up and try to acquire Paradise by fulfilling your prayer duty.' If a person, a true believer, gets up and does his or her ablution and afterward performs the duty, all his or her sins are forgiven between the times of the daily prayers."

HOW DO YOU RECOGNIZE?

One day our dear Prophet and his Companions were having a conversation. The Messenger was talking about the Judgment Day. One of his Companions asked: "How will you recognize the *ummah* on that dreadful day?"

He answered: "Imagine one of you has many horses and some of them are black and some are white. Do you feel difficulty in distinguishing them from each other?"

They said: "No, it would be very easy."

The dear Prophet said: "The parts of your body that you clean in your ablution will be snow-white on that day and they will be recognized easily. I will wait for you in front of the Kawthar Pool, the source of which will never end, but not all of you will be able to reach me. I will ask the angels why some of you cannot enter Paradise and meet with me. The angels will respond: "They haven't kept their promises after you and they went into sins and they didn't pray regularly."

AFTER AN EVENING PRAYER

After having the evening prayer performed, the Prophet went to his home to perform the *Awwabin* prayer which is accepted as a very precious worship. Some of his friends stayed in the Masjid. After a while, the Prophet came back to the Masjid out of breath upon which his friends came towards him full of curiosity to learn the reason of his coming back.

He said: "I have got some good news. God opened one of the doors of the heavens. He is all proud of you and is mentioning to the angels about you. He says: Look at My servants. They have performed their evening prayer and they are waiting for the next prayer in the mosque."

The Prophet said: "If one of you continues his evening prayer after performing the obligatory cycles, he or she is named among the people of *awwabin* (those who repent)."

6 cycles of prayer after the obligatory 3 cycles of the Evening Prayer is very precious for God. He then uttered the verse: "*Your Lord best knows what is in your souls (in respect of all matters, including what you think of your parents). If you are righteous (in your thoughts and deeds), then surely He is All-Forgiving to those who turn to Him in humble contrition.*" (Al-Isra, 17:25).

PROSTRATING A LOT…

Ibn Ka'b al-Aslami narrates: "I spent my night with the Messenger. I helped him with some things such as bringing him water for ablution."

He said: "Wish from me whatever you like."

I said: "I wish we will be together in Paradise."

He said: "Anything other than this?"

I said: "Nothing more"

He said: "Then help me by prostrating a lot."

GOOD DEEDS WHICH REMOVE BAD ONES….

Umar and his friends were having a conversation one day. He performed ablution and said: "I saw the Messenger perform ablution like me. I clearly remember his words afterwards." He said: "If someone performs ablution like me and performs his or her midday prayer, God cleans his or her sins committed between the morning and the midday. When he or she performs his or her mid-afternoon prayer, God cleans the sins committed between the midday and mid-afternoon. If he or she continues to the evening prayer then God cleans the sins committed between the mid-afternoon and the evening. Eventually, when he or she performs the night prayer, God cleans the sins committed between the evening and the night. These are the good deeds which remove the bad ones."

HOW CAN WE EXPLAIN THAT ALL THE WORSHIPS ARE INCLUDED IN THE DAILY PRAYERS?

Just as a human being is a small example of the universe, the *surah* Fatiha is a small example of the Qur'an which includes the major principles of it.

The daily prayer (*salah*) includes all the worships in it. For instance, it includes fasting because you cannot eat or drink anything during a prayer. It includes the compulsory alms giving (*zakat*) because it is one's lifetime's alms giving. It includes the religious pilgrimage duty (the *Hajj*) because you turn your face to the Ka'ba which is the center of circumambulation (*tawaf*). Some angels worship only by saying "*La ilahe illallah*" (There is no deity but Allah) and some just say "*Allahu Akbar*" (God is the greatest) and others utter the word "*Subhanallah*" (Glory be to God). The prayer includes all these words.

On the other hand, the prayer includes the worshipping ways of other creatures. Mountains stand just as we stand in the prayer. Animals wait just as we bow in the prayer. Birds fly together in groups just as we group together with a congregation in prayer.

MAN OF PRAYER

We can wait in prostration without saying even a word, for as long as we desire. We can utter some verses in the prayer, sometimes which take us into different worlds. This is up to the person who is praying. Our Prophet's prostration time equaled the time he spent in bowing and standing in the prayer. He uttered the *surah* of Al-Baqarah, Al-Imran and An-Nisa during his standing time in the prayer. However, to us, it seems like a very long time when we spend two or three minutes in standing in our prayers!

YOUR PRAYER TIME IS PASSING

Abu Yazid (Bayazid) al-Bistami, one of the greatest Sufi masters, stayed asleep one night and the time for the morning prayer had passed. When he woke up, he realized that the morning had already arrived. He was profoundly sorry and he felt miserable since he missed his prayer.

He performed the prayer at a later time after the sunrise. As he was in prostration, he heard some voice which said: "O Bayazid, your repentance was accepted. And because of your deep repentance, you were given the good deeds equaled to 70.000 prayers."

He was relieved upon hearing this. After a few months, he was sleeping again through a morning prayer. However, he was woken up by the Satan this time.

Bayazid was shocked to be woken up by the Satan and he asked him curiously: "O cursed Satan, this is an unusual thing to be woken up by you. I know obviously that you must have a penetrating idea in doing this."

The Satan answered: "When you missed a morning prayer a few months ago you felt such a deep repentance that it caused the heavens to tremble. Upon that, you were given much more reward. This time I don't want you to have such good deeds so I woke you up."

IN THE LAST MINUTE

A scene from the time of the Judgment Day

Everywhere was full of people in the area of the judgment. Some people were in shock, others were looking around without moving even slightly, still others were waiting kneeled down, and between their hands were their heads. He was sweating chills running up and down. When he was in the world, he heard a lot about the Judgment Day. Yet, he would never think it would be such a horrifying day. Everybody was waiting his or her turn to account for what he or she did in the world. He heard his name being announced. He was shocked to hear his name and he went to where he was called. He walked through the crowd and he came somewhere which seemed to be the center. He was walking headlong. All his life flashed before his eyes and he said "Thanks be to God" and continued: "The family into which I was born was a very pious one. My father spent all his money for the sake of God. My mother was like him. I tried to be like them. I performed my daily prayers, I fasted, and I did all the necessary things for my religious duty."

Tears were pouring from his eyes and he said: "I love my Creator, God. At least, I feel so. On the other hand, he thought it was impossible to gain Paradise without God's forgiveness and mercy."

The time for his account was passing very slowly and he was sweating. He was waiting for the result. The responsible angels came and took him. They were about to tell him the result. Meanwhile, he was very nervous and virtually was about to collapse to the ground due to his anxiety. A roar arose from the crowd and his name was read among the ones deserving of Hell.

He kneeled down and he was flabbergasted. He started to run to the right and to the left. He thought: I consumed all my breath for the sake of God. I did all the things for my religion. This cannot happen. This is impossible. Two angels took him to the way of Hell. He exerted every effort to get rid of them but it was all in vain. He begged for mercy. He said: "What about my prayers, my reading Qur'an? Isn't there anything which can save me from Hell?"

They came very closer to the flames. He again shouted out: "What about my daily prayers? My prayers, help me…Please my prayers, help me…My prayers…"

The angels did not stop and continued to Hell. They came to Hell. He turned and looked back the last and for all. All his hopes came to an end.

One of the angels hit him and he started falling to Hell. After he went down a few meters, a hand held him and took him out of the hole. It was an old man.

He asked: "Who are you?"

The old man smiled and said: "I am your daily prayers."

He said: "Why are you so late? I begged for you to save me. Why did you wait?"

The old man said: "You always delayed me to the last minutes. Did you remember?"

When he opened his eyes, he was lying in his bed. He said: "Thank God, it was all a dream. Then he heard the night *adhan*, he shot ahead to perform his ablution.

THE PRAYER PERFORMED IN THE PRISON

Abdullah ibn Tahir, the governor of Horasan province, was a very fair and just man. The soldiers had caught some thieves and they brought them to the governor. While the thieves were being taken to the prison, one of them ran away. The soldiers caught another man on the street thinking he was the fugitive. But in fact, he was just a blacksmith going to his home.

The innocent blacksmith performed his ablution and started his night prayer in the prison begging God for his innocence to be revealed. He was pouring tears and praying saying "O my Lord, You know I am innocent, please help me to prove my innocence."

The governor ordered the soldiers to keep them in the prison at night. During the night, while sleeping, he dreamed of some four people who took his reign over. He sweated chills and woke up all of a sudden. When he slept again, he dreamed the same things. He called the manager of the

prison to his home and asked: "Is there anyone who is inno-cent in the prison?"

The manager said: "I cannot know this, sir. But, there is someone who is always praying and crying."

The governor ordered his man to take the man to his home. The soldiers took the blacksmith to the governor.

The governor said to the blacksmith: "Please forgive me, and accept this gold as a present and an apology. And when-ever you wish something, come to me, I can give whatever you want."

The blacksmith said: "I accept your apology and gift but I cannot come to you whenever I wish something. God saved me from many dangerous situations when I prayed to Him af-ter my prayers. He is the Most Compassionate and the Merci-ful so I cannot leave Him and go to anyone else. He is the only one who can give all my desires."

THE GUIDING LIGHTS

✤ If you love God, you must undoubtedly be sure that He loves you. If you do not carry the love of God in your heart then it can be said that you are not appreciated by Him.

✤ Each sort of worship should solely be devoted to God and not anything else.

✤ No daily engagement is more important than the prayer for a Muslim. The prayer time should be a daily calendar for a true believer.

✤ Our attitudes reflect our religion so we must be very cautious about them.

✤ Those who are passionate of prayer don't leave the prayer time to the last minute.

✤ The daily prayer is to get in touch with God in one aspect so you should always be cautious during the prayer with the realization of being known by Him all the time.

✤ One cannot get rid of ignorance without knowing the religious requirements.

✤ Daily prayer is such an important duty that even a war cannot be counted as an excuse for its passing.

✤ If you do not struggle for feeling the prayer deeply, it is certain that you are unable to feel it as it deserves.

✤ Each sin opens a door to the new one.

✤ If your nights are all passing without prayers, you cannot feed others for a long time.

✤ There is a strong relation between the target and the way, with which we can reach it, so being serious on the way of the target is very important.

✤ Being serious is one of the indicators of being a true Muslim.

✤ Appreciating the things which are esteemed by God is one if the important conditions of being a devoted Muslim.

✤ While levity is an indicator of being far away from God, seriousness shows one's closeness to God.

✤ Those who don't attach importance to their defects can never recover their faults.

✤ Living with the beauties of the future is an elixir diminishing the pains of the past.

✤ If you are content with only God and His knowing of you and if you don't attach importance to be known by the public, one day your name is written on the heavens and you are known by the all angels.

✤ Our Prophet always taught us to have goals and encouraged us for having goals in life.

✤ A nation's rising and falling depends on the education of its youth.

✤ If you want to foretell about a nation's future, turn your eyes to its youth and their education then your foresight would be certain.

SERIOUSNESS, PIETY AND DIGNITY

FROM THE QUR'AN

O you who believe! Be upholders and standard-bearers of right for God's sake, being witnesses for (the establishment of) absolute justice. And by no means let your detestation for a people (or their detestation for you) move you to (commit the sin of) deviating from justice. Be just: this is nearer and more suited to righteousness and piety. Seek righteousness and piety, and always act in reverence for God. Surely God is fully aware of all that you do. (Al-Ma'idah, 5:8).

The Paradise promised to the God-revering, pious ones can be likened to a garden through which rivers flow. Its produce is everlasting, and so its shade. That is the ultimate outcome for those who keep from disobedience to God in reverence for Him and piety, just as the ultimate outcome for the unbelievers is the Fire. (Ar-Ra'd, 13:35).

FROM THE LAST MESSENGER

The last Messenger of God said: "Be afraid of God wherever you are, do a good deed after a sin which will clean it, treat people morally upright."

"The clever is the one who accounts himself or herself for his actions before he or she dies, the weak is the one who is enthusiastic about Paradise though excessively fond of transient pleasures of this material world."

"Undoubtedly, God forgives what you are thinking in your mind on the condition that you don't put it into action."

THIS IS THE STATE'S CANDLE

Umar, the Caliph, was working in his office room one day. A candle was burning on his table. Meanwhile, Abdurrahman ibn Awf came to visit him. He gave his regards but the Caliph did not answer.

After a while, the Caliph blew out the candle and burned another one and answered his regards. Abdurrahman ibn Awf asked the reason for his delay in answering.

The Caliph said: "The first was the state's candle so it would be unsuitable to conduct my personal affairs under its light. This candle is mine so I can do my own actions with this."

PRAYER

FROM THE QUR'AN

And when (O Messenger) My servants ask you about Me, then surely I am near: I answer the prayer of the suppliant when he prays to Me. So let them respond to My call (without hesitation), and believe and trust in Me (in the way required of them), so that they may be guided to spiritual and intellectual excellence and right conduct. (Al-Baqarah, 2:186).

Do you not see that all that is in the heavens and the earth, and the birds flying in patterned ranks with wings spread out glorify God. Each knows the way of its prayer and glorification. God has full knowledge of all that they do. (An-Nur, 24:41).

FROM THE LAST MESSENGER

The last Messenger of God said: "There is no worship more precious than prayer in the presence of God."

"For whoever the door of prayer is opened, the door of mercy is as well. The thing that God loves most is to demand health and happiness from Him. Destiny can only be changed through prayer. So you should attach importance to prayer."

"If one of you prays for your Muslim brother or sister, the angels say: 'Amen, we wish the same thing for you.'"

"Your prostrating is the time in which you are the closest to God, so pray a lot while prostrating."

THE PRAYER OF THE LAST MESSENGER

"O God, I demand your protection from meanness, cowardice, becoming infirm by old age, disharmony in the world and sufferings of the grave."

THREE POINTS

The last Messenger of God said: "Whoever wants his prayer to be accepted, he should pray a lot during his comfortable time. If your desire is not a sin or bad relation with your relatives, there are three points in your demand; the first is that your demand is accepted immediately and you are given whatever you want, the second is that God keeps your demand for a time when you are really and desperately in need, the third is God protects you from a bad incident which is going to befall you."

His Companions said: "Then we shall pray a lot."

He said: "Pray and demand how much you can, because God's treasure of mercy is infinite."

THE SUNSET HOUR (*IFTAR*) DURING RAMADAN

Our dear Prophet said: "The prayer of someone that is fasting is not denied."

Our Prophet prayed in this way: "O God, I fasted just for your sake! I finished my fasting with the food you have given. I solely trust You! I believe in you! I mean to fast tomorrow. Please, forgive my all sins in the past and the future! O God, forgive me and all my Muslim brothers and sisters during the Judgment Day!"

THE PRAYER OF THE PROPHET JONAH

Our Prophet said: "If those who are miserable pray like my brother Jonah, God answers and accepts their prayers: '*There is no deity but You, All-Glorified You are. Surely, I have been one of the wrongdoers.*'"

PRAYERS FROM THE HEART

O God, teach us where, what and how to speak! Do not leave us alone even for a second! O God, you know my need and I just demand You from You! O God, please enrich my heart in order to know You better! I desire not to be a known person but to be your lover! O God, direct me according to your desire not mine! O God, if the things you have given to me will direct my way to the bad, I do not want them!

THE GUIDING LIGHTS

❧ It doesn't matter how much big the sins you have committed, God's mercy is always bigger.

❧ The biggest loss is the idea of giving up prayer.

❧ Making an excuse after committing a sin is another sin. Repentance and being determined not to do it again is the right thing to do.

❧ Attaching importance to the prayer means attaching importance to God's presence.

❧ Prayer lacking in earnestness is disrespectfulness towards God, one should be very earnest while praying and open his or her heart while opening his or her hands.

❧ As bread and water is a necessity for the body, prayer is the same for the soul.

❧ The biggest prayer is to lock oneself to the target you believe.

❧ Those who are in love with God are never satisfied with prayer.

❧ The one who committed a big sin and always feels guilty in the presence of God is better than the one who commits small sins but is indifferent to them.

❧ If God didn't want to bestow, He would not have given the feeling of demanding.

❧ Suffering is the leading prayer.

❧ You should perform a fast of sin and even a small one should not break it.

RESPECT TO PARENTS AND MAINTAINING BONDS OF KINSHIP

FROM THE QUR'AN

Your Lord has decreed that you worship none but Him alone, and treat parents with the best of kindness. Should one of them, or both, attain old age in your lifetime, do not say "Ugh!" to them (as an indication of complaint or impatience), nor push them away; and always address them in gracious words. Lower to them the wing of humility out of mercy, and say: "My Lord, have mercy on them even as they cared for me in childhood." Your Lord best knows what is in your souls (in respect of all matters, including what you think of your parents). If you are righteous (in your thoughts and deeds), then surely He is All-Forgiving to those who turn to Him in humble contrition. (Al-Isra, 17:23–25).

FROM THE LAST MESSENGER

The last Messenger of God said: "Whoever wants his or her livelihood to be enriched by God, and to have longer lifetime shall visit their parents and make them happy."

"God's consent with you depends on your father's consent, and God's discontent is up to your father's."

"The best of you is the one who behaves to his or her family kindly. I am the best one in this respect."

MOTHER AND FATHER

Parents should be highly venerated as they are considered respected in our religion. If you show disrespect to them it is tantamount to being disrespectful to God. If you treat them badly, it is undoubtedly certain that you will be mistreated in the future. You should always keep in mind that you have been a burden to them since the time you were born. They got up many times for you in the middle of the night. They did not live for themselves but just for you, especially for the first periods of your life.

In this respect, if you hold them in high esteem you are just doing what you should do. Humanly, they deserve to be respected because their self sacrificing cannot be criticized. You may be considered as fortunate, if you can show them great respect when they are alive. It is unfortunate of you, if you neglect them in their lives.

In today's world, unfortunately, it is not only those who maintain an irreligious life but those who claim to be pious are behaving disrespectfully towards their parents.

Children should venerate their parents, however, their parents, in turn, should teach them the necessities of the contemporary world while not neglecting to empower their souls with the teachings of the religion. It is a sort of ignorance not to take into consideration the children's bilateral education.

Family is the basic structure of a nation. The more family members show the essential respect to each other, the more the nation becomes a peaceful place.

DON'T FORGET THE NEEDLE

There was a mother with two children living in a small village in Turkey. She was loved very much by her neighbors and children as she was very kind towards them. Her name was Güllü. Her children's names were Safiye and Selim. Safiye was generally at home helping her mom with the house chores. Selim, her son, had a bed wetting problem. Since he was too old to have such a problem, he was very ashamed in the morning. But his mother, Güllü, never humiliated him for this.

Güllü was a very pious woman. She was very afraid of committing sins especially seizing someone's right wrongfully.

One day, she took a needle from one of her neighbors. In her life time, she always avoided misappropriation. She promised her neighbor to bring it back when she completed her job.

Days passed; however, she forgot to bring the needle back. One day, all of a sudden, she died. Her children and husband were all were miserable and couldn't believe her death.

After her death, all the house chores were left to Safiye, her daughter. Selim was very anxious from then on, because he was very ashamed of his bed wetting problem. He thought his sister would get angry with him for his problem.

Days passed, one morning Selim turned out the way he feared. His bed was again wet. However, her sister wasn't angry with him as taught by her mom and solved the problem by washing it immediately.

One day, their father's shirt was torn. He gave it to his daughter to sew. She said she would sew it immediately but she couldn't find a needle. She checked the entire house but in vain. Her father said "We can buy it tomorrow from the store, my dear daughter, so there is no need to look for it."

When Safiye slept, she had a dream of her mother. She got very excited and her mother said to her in her dream: "The needle is on the oven. After using it, please give it to our neighbor my dear. "

She got up out of the blue and went to the kitchen and saw the needle on the oven. She was flabbergasted and right away she woke her father up.

She told about her dream and the story touched the father. He tried hard to keep his tears but he failed.

Safiye took the needle to her neighbor in the morning and she was certain that her mother was relieved upon handing in the needle.

YOUNG ANIMALS

Each young animal is born in need of great care. They are weak and incapable of caring for themselves. The feeling of tenderness of the parents constitutes the patience necessary for feeding and bringing up the young animals. This sort of tender feeling does not come out until the female gives birth. This feeling has been bestowed for all creatures including human beings.

When a young animal opens its eyes to the earth, it finds its parents with him. If not, staying alive would be almost impossible for it. By the way, all the essential food for it is ready to be sucked from its mother.

The feeling of tenderness of the parents makes us feel the compassion of God, the source of everything in the known and the unknown universe.

For instance, a kangaroo, only one centimeter long and one gram in weight, is born into its mother's bag. None of its organs has completed its development yet. It cannot even see and hear. However, it finds its food ready to eat in the bag of its mother.

There are four different milk sources in the mother's bag. Each has got milk different in thickness according to the age of the young animal.

The young animal feeds from the breast which is suitable to its age. Before a young animal leaves the bag, a newborn young may arrive at the bag. This newly-born one uses another breast suitable for itself without bothering its brother or sister.

Sharks and dolphins get the essential food for themselves under the water. Their young suck the mothers under the water. However, it seems impossible to get the milk of the mother without swallowing the sea water. Hence, the mother spurts the milk into the young's mouth as it was taught and thus preventing the young from drinking sea water.

As it is clear from the lives of the animals, each species has food ready and essential for its life in the world and this food is submitted to him in the best way, through the infinite mercy and compassion of God.

FASTING

FROM THE QUR'AN

O you who believe! Prescribed for you is the Fast, as it was prescribed for those before you, so that you may deserve God's protection (against the temptations of your carnal soul) and attain piety. (Fasting is for) a fixed number of days. If any of you is so ill that he cannot fast, or on a journey, he must fast the same number of other days. But for those who can no longer manage to fast, there is a redemption (penance) by feeding a person in destitution (for each day missed, or giving him the same amount in money). Yet better it is for him who volunteers greater good (by either giving more, or fasting in case of recovery), and that you should fast (when you are able to) is better for you, if you but knew (the worth of fasting). The month of Ramadan, in which the Qur'an was sent down as guidance for people, and as clear signs of Guidance and the Criterion (between truth and falsehood). Therefore whoever of you is present this month must fast it, and whoever is so ill that he cannot fast or is on a journey (must fast the same) number of other days. God wills ease for you, and He does not will hardship for you, so that you can complete the number of the days required, and exalt God for He has guided you, and so it may be that you will give thanks (due to Him). (Al-Baqarah, 2:183–185).

FROM THE LAST MESSENGER

I am fasting...

The Last Messenger of God said: "If one of you does not stop lying or bad behavior towards other people while fasting should know the fact that God does not need his or her hunger. You should never treat other people badly or say any bad words to them, especially, while fasting. And, if someone provokes and treats you badly just say 'I am fasting' to them."

Our dear Prophet said: "If one of you leaves fasting in Ramadan without any acceptable excuse, he or she undoubtedly should know the fact that no day other than Ramadan is as precious as a day in Ramadan for fasting. He or she cannot get the same reward even if he or she fasts until the end of his or her life."

A SERVANT WHO THANKS ALLAH A LOT

Our dear Prophet was in his room with his wife Aisha on the 15th night of Sha'ban, the night of Barat. He rested for while in his bed and then got up silently. Aisha looked for him in the room without lighting a candle. Her hand touched the Prophet and she realized he was in prostration. Our dear Prophet was praying without raising his head from the ground. Aisha, the mother of all Muslims, tried to hear his words in order to keep them and tell it to the other Muslims. This continued till the morning.

In the morning Aisha asked the Prophet: "O God's Messenger, why are you getting yourself tired so much as God has already forgiven you. You don't need that much worship."

The Messenger said: "Shall I not be a thankful servant of God? And do you know the importance of this night?"

Aisha said: "I really do not know what the secret of tonight."

The Messenger said: "All the babies who are to be born this year are indicated and written tonight. And, all the people who are going to die inside this year are indicated and written tonight, as well. All livelihoods are allotted tonight. All the good deeds and the bad ones are taken in the presence of God tonight. All people can only enter Paradise by the compassion of God not by their good deeds."

Aisha asked: "Even you?"

The Prophet said: "Yes, even me, I am no exception."

WHAT IS THE REASON?

Aisha narrates: "I have never witnessed the Prophet to be fasting all the month except Ramadan. He also fasted more in Sha'ban when compared to the other months."

Usamah asked the reason for this to the Messenger and he said: "Sha'ban is the month that most people are negligent about. Sha'ban is the month in which all the deeds of the people are raised to the presence of God and I want my deeds to reach Him while I am fasting."

HE USED TO DO THAT

One day Masruk said to Aisha: "There were two persons from the Companions of the Prophet who never hesitated to help the others in need. The first of the two was always in hurry to break his fast and to perform his evening prayer but the other was unlike him."

Aisha said: What is the first one's name?

Masruk answered: "Abdullah."

Aisha, the mother of Muslims, said: "The Messenger of God used to do like him. He broke his fast with a fresh date and if he couldn't find the fresh one, he preferred dry dates or some water to break the fast."

THE DOOR OF RAYYAN

The Prophet said: "There is a door in Paradise called Rayyan and through which only the performers of fast enter Paradise."

THE NIGHT OF REGAIB

Our dear Prophet said: "God awards the ones in three ways who fast in the month Rajab. He forgives their past bad deeds and protects them for the rest of their lives. And they do not feel thirsty during the frightful Day of Judgment."

An old person arose from the crowd and said: "O Messenger of God, I am not healthy enough to fast one month."

Upon this, God's Messenger said: "You can fast on the first, the fifteenth, and the last day of Rajab. If so, you may be regarded as though you have fasted the entire month. By the way, do not be unaware of the first Friday's night of Rajab. Because all angels descend down in the third part of the night and gather around the Ka'ba. God says to them: "Wish from me whatever you like." The angels answer: "We beg for the forgiveness of the fasting performers in the month Rajab."

God says: "I have forgiven them all."

THE NIGHT OF BARAT

Our Prophet said: "When you reach the fifteenth night of Sha'ban, that is Barat, spend its night with prayer and the day with fasting. Undoubtedly, God expects our prayers during the night and He says: "Is there anyone who wants to be forgiven? Is there anyone who wants to earn livelihood? Is there anyone who wants health and happiness? I will give all those desires tonight."

FASTING ALL YEAR

Our dear Prophet said: "If you fast during Ramadan and add to it six days in the month of Shawwal, the month following Ramadan, you are considered as you have fasted all year."

THE RAMADAN FESTIVAL

On the first night of Ramadan, God views people. He spares many people from the punishment of Hell during Ramadan. On the 29th night of the Ramadan, He spares as many people as He has spared to that night. Angels tremble with excitement on the day of the Ramadan festival. God manifests Himself with a light unprecedented before. While people are enjoying themselves with conversations among their friends on the first day of the Ramadan festival, some angels say: "What is the award of an employee when he has completed his task without a fault?"

Other angels answer: "He gets his complete charge."

And God says: "I hold you as a witness that I have forgiven all the full fasting performers on Ramadan."

THE GUIDING LIGHTS

❀ Servitude is made up of sincere intention and action which supports it.

❀ A person may not be willing to worship all the time, but the important thing is to struggle to do so.

❀ Knowledge reaches its true value by means of worship.

❀ Solid character, which never changes even if the conditions are unstable, is important but to continue it is more important.

❀ God has many blessings upon His servants (people) but the most important of them is to be aware of His blessings.

❀ Only the patients know the true value of being healthy.

❀ Though food and beverages are physical nutrients, their relation with the soul cannot be denied.

❀ Eating and sleeping little is indispensible to reach spiritual maturity.

❀ Words may be deceitful but the attitudes and unchanging behaviors may not.

❀ Those who do not want to experience failure should always consult with the experienced.

❀ There is no self-trust in Islam, we should only trust in God and use the will power given by Him in a good way.

❀ Reaching spiritual maturity requires your thoughts to be dependent on the existence of Islam.

❀ One of the crucial features of sincerity is to act reasonably.

❀ Writhing for the "remedy" opens a door for the solution.

SECRECY AND CONSULTATION

FROM THE QUR'AN

The route (of blame and retaliation) is only against those who wrong people and behave rebelliously on earth, offending against all right. For such there is a painful punishment. (Ash-Shura 42:38).

FROM THE LAST MESSENGER

Souls

Our Prophet said: "Souls are like the gathered groups, from them the ones who met before become close friends, and the ones not so draw apart."

A SECRET THAT BELONGS
TO THE PROPHET

Anas told one of his friends, Thabit: "One day, after completing my chore, I left the Prophet's room as I thought he would rest for a short time during the noon. I saw some children playing on the street and the Messenger came and gave his regards to the kids. Then the Prophet sent me to do something which was a secret between him and me. I never revealed this secret to anyone and I still keep it with me."

PRESCRIBED PURIFYING ALMS AND CHARITY

FROM THE QUR'AN

Establish the Prayer, and pay the Prescribed Purifying Alms (the *Zakah*); and bow (in the Prayer, not by forming a different community or congregation, but) together with those who bow (the Muslims). (Al-Baqarah, 2:43).

Your guardian and confidant is none but God, and His Messenger, and those who, having believed, establish the Prayer in conformity with all its conditions, and pay the Prescribed Purifying Alms (the *Zakah*), and they bow (in humility and submission to Him). (Al-Maidah, 5:55).

The Prescribed Purifying Alms (the *Zakah*) are meant only for the poor, and the destitute (albeit, out of self-respect, they do not give the impression that they are in need), and those in charge of collecting (and administering) them, and those whose hearts are to be won over (for support of God's cause, including those whose hostility is to be prevented), and to free those in bondage (slavery and captivity), and to help those over-burdened with debt, and in God's cause (to exalt God's word, to provide for the warriors and students, and to help the pilgrims), and for the wayfarer (in need of help). This is an ordinance from God. God is All-Knowing, All-Wise. (At-Toubah, 9:60).

(Those) who break God's covenant after its solemn binding, and sever the bonds God commanded to be joined, and cause disorder and corruption on earth. Such are those who are the losers (in both this world and the next). (Al-Baqarah, 2:27).

FROM THE LAST MESSENGER

For the sake of God

Our dear Prophet said: "The one who loves or hates someone for the sake of God and who expends or is thrifty for the sake of God has completed his or her belief."

More Favorable

Our dear Prophet said: "The one who does not avoid giving alms is more favorable than those who take it. Start giving alms from the ones who are closest to you in relative relations. The best alms are the one given from the properties that you are not in need. If a person wants to be virtuous and honest, God will make him or her virtuous. If a person does not expect anything from someone else, God will not leave him or her in need."

I WANT TO BE RICH

There was a Muslim called Salaba from Medina. Salaba was fed up with poverty. He wanted to be rich as soon as possible. He thought that the best solution was to have the blessings of our Prophet and so he came to him and said: "O God's Messenger, pray to God to make me rich."

Our Prophet said: "O Salaba, a little wealth for which you can show gratitude is much better than a great deal of wealth for which you are not grateful."

Salaba thought of the words of our Prophet. Is poverty more favorable for himself? He thought that it must have been true as our Prophet gave this advice instead of his prayer. Afterwards, the worldly desires tempted him and he came to our Prophet again and said: "O my Prophet, pray for me to be rich."

This time our Prophet said: "Am I not a convenient model for you? I swear that the mountains would have followed me as gold or silver if I had wanted; however I did not want it."

Nonetheless Salaba insisted: "I swear that I will protect the poor if God makes me rich and I will give the rights of the holders."

Then, our Prophet prayed: "O God! May You make Salaba gain what he desires."

From then on, Salaba began to raise sheep. Then, the number of the sheep increased to the degree that makes many herds. As Salaba performed his prayer with a congregation, he was called the bird of mosque but from then on he could perform only noon and afternoon prayer with a congregation. He dealt with his sheep in the other prayers' time and he sometimes did not perform his prayers.

After a short period of time, his herds of sheep could not fit into the pasture of Medina. He needed to go to far deserts and well-watered plateaus, and from then on he could only be seen in Friday prayer. At last, he forgot the Friday prayer and our Prophet asked: "Where is Salaba?"

The Companions answered: "He is following around his sheep in the deserts because his sheep cannot fit into here."

Our Prophet said: "What a pity!"

When the alms verse was sent, rich Muslims gave the one fortieth of their incomes as alms willingly. However, Salaba said to the people coming to want his alms: "This is protection money" and he did not give anything to them. Our Prophet got upset when he heard it and repeated his word: "What a pity!"

Therefore, God sent theseverses:

Among them are some who vowed to God: "Surely, if God grants us out of His grace and bounty, we will most certainly (pay the Prescribed Alms and) spend in alms for His sake, and we will most certainly be among the righteous." Then God granted them out of His grace and bounty, but they clung to it in niggardly fashion and turned about, swerving away (from what they had vowed). So as a consequence He has caused hypocrisy to be in their hearts (and to remain rooted therein) until the day when they will meet Him (at death), because they have broken their word to God that they promised Him, and because they were lying habitually. (At-Toubah, 9:75–77).

When one of Salaba's relatives heard the verse, he went to Salaba and said: "I wouldn't have expected this from you! God sent verses about you."

The moment Salaba learned this, he immediately went to our Prophet and wanted him to accept his alms, but he said: "I was banned to accept your alms by God."

He was so sorry that he threw a handful of soil into his head and our Prophet said: "You harmed yourself. I said to you before but you did not pay any attention to me."

He did not want to take his alms and he accepted nothing from Salaba. When Abu Bakr became a Caliph, Salaba went to him and said: "You know my position in the presence of our dear Prophet and among Ansar (the Helpers, Madinan believers); please accept my alms."

Abu Bakr said: "I cannot accept what our Prophet did not accept."

Abu Bakr also didn't accept his alms until his death. When Umar became a Caliph, Salaba came to him again and said: "The ruler of the Muslims! Accept my alms."

Umar replied: "I cannot accept your alms which our Prophet and Abu Bakr did not accept."

Umar also did not accept his alms until his death. When Uthman became a Caliph, this time Salaba came to Uthman and wanted Uthman to accept his alms but Uthman rejected it and said: "I cannot accept what our Prophet, Abu Bakr, Umar did not accept."

After a period of time, Salaba died in the period when Uthman was a Caliph.

A LOAN IS BETTER THAN CHARITY

Our Prophet saw a word which was written on the gate of Paradise on the night of the Miraj: "Alms will be rewarded ten times but a loan will be rewarded eighteen times."

Our Prophet said: "O Gabriel! Why is a loan better than alms?"

Then Gabriel said: "Because a beggar may demand money even if he has money with him but the one who demands loan demands it because of his need."

SHORTCUT WAY

A group of people were talking to the famous scholar, Abu Said, and they were listening to his advice, when one of them asked: "O Abu Said! What is the way of God's acceptance?"

Abu Said answered: "My brother! There are many ways leading us to God's acceptance but the easiest and shortest one is to not leave people in a difficult condition and to help them when required."

ABUNDANCE OF ALMS

Our Prophet explained an event: "A man who was passing through a desert heard that a cloud said, "Water the garden of a certain man!" then, that cloud went to a dark and stony place and poured its water there. The man saw the water being stored in a river and followed the water and he saw that a man was watering his garden by directing water to specific points of his garden with an oar. The man asked: "What is your name?"

That man watering his garden said the name which the other man heard from the cloud. The man asked: "Why do you ask my name?"

He said: "I have heard your name from that cloud and a voice saying: 'Water the garden of a certain man'. What do you do to be the object of this honor?"

The owner of the garden said: "As you are curious about it, then I will tell you. I account the production of this garden and I deliver one third of it as alms, I eat one third of it with my children and I put aside one third of it as seed."

DISTINCTION OF THE LAWFUL AND UNLAWFUL, LOYALTY AND FIDELITY

FROM THE QUR'AN

So (O people) partake as pure, lawful and wholesome of what God has provided you, and give thanks for His bounty, if it is indeed Him that you worship. (An-Nahl, 16:114).

In consequence God will reward the truthful ones for having been true to their covenant, and punish the hypocrites if He wills or turn to them in lenience and accept their repentance (if they repent). Surely God is All-Forgiving, All-Compassionate. (Al-Ahzab, 33:24).

The Word of your Lord (which He sent down in parts in different periods considering the conditions of each period) is perfected (with the Qur'an) as the embodiment of truth (with respect to the essentials of belief, principles of worship and good conduct, the rules to govern human life, and all the tidings it gives considering the past and future including the Hereafter), and of justice (regarding all the commandments it contains): there is no altering of His words (the laws He has established for life, and the operation of the universe; attempting to interfere with them will bring about great disasters, so no one must ever attempt to change His commandments, which are contained in the Book). He is the All-Hearing, the All-Knowing (Who knows every need of every creature, every requirement of every age, just as He knows how you respond to His commandments). (Al-An'am, 6:115).

FROM THE LAST MESSENGER

Loyalty

The Messenger of God said: "O people! Always keep in your mind that, if you become unfaithful to your words and to the others in this life, all your unfaithfulness will be uncovered in detail in the next world."

Trust

The Messenger of God said: "If you have no trust, you have no faith; it means you do not have a complete and real faith. It is difficult to find a strong concept of trust out of faithful people. If you are sure about yourself and trust, you are a real Muslim and vice versa."

HOW IS THE PROPHET?

Once the Prophet was talking with a group of people in which Abu Bakr was also present in Arqam's house. Abu Bakr wanted Islam to be announced publicly and he insisted on it.

On his insistence, God's Messenger accepted and they all went to the Ka'ba. They resided in the Ka'ba. On the other side, Abu Jahil, Abu Sufyan, and Utba ibn Rabi'ah, who disliked and hated the Messenger of God and Muslims, were sitting together. They were very surprised when they saw the Muslims in a group. They could not understand what was going on.

Meanwhile, Abu Bakr stood up and wanted them to give up their idols and believe in God and the Messenger. After hearing these words, those mischief makers got annoyed, insulted, and attacked Abu Bakr and the Muslims. The Muslims, without thinking and caring for themselves first, immediately saved God's Messenger. Some unfortunate mischief makers beat him; especially Utba ibn Rabi'ah kicked him with his ironed shoes. Abu Bakr's face was deeply injured.

Some men from Abu Bakr's tribe (the Banu Taym) heard this incident and came to save Abu Bakr. They carried him in a cloth to his home. At first, his relatives thought that he would lose his life. They got annoyed so much that they came back to the Ka'ba and said to mischief makers: "If Abu Bakr dies, be sure that we will kill Utba, too."

All his relatives gathered and began to wait. Abu Bakr was sleeping in his bed unconsciously. He was able to open his eyes in the evening and merely said: "How is God's Messenger?"

All his relatives were shocked against this question and asked him angrily: "You almost died because of him and you are still asking about him!"

His mother Ummul Khayr was waiting with grumbling eyes and asked him: "What do you want to eat?"

He wanted nothing to eat and asked about God's Messenger again. He tried to stand up but he could not manage to do so. He wanted his mother to go to Umm Jamil, the sister of Umar ibn al-Khattab, to learn how God's Messenger was.

His mother went to Umm Jamil and asked about the Prophet. Umm Jamil said: "I do not know how God's Messenger is, by the way, why does your son ask about him?"

Umm Jamil wanted to visit Abu Bakr and went with Ummul Khayr. Umm Jamil found Abu Bakr in a very suffering situation. He wished God to punish that tribe.

Abu Bakr again asked God's Messenger to Umm Jamil. Umm Jamil clearly said that he was alive and well.

Abu Bakr again asked about God's Messenger but this time to learn about his place. Ummu Jamil answered the question saying he is well at Arqam's home. Abu Bakr said: "It is impossible for me to eat and drink without seeing him well."

Ummul Khayr obviously understood his son's feelings and that he would not be relieved if he does not see the Messenger of God and said: "My dear son, we will take you to him when the entire city is asleep."

When evening arrived and silence fell down upon the city, Umm Jamil and Ummul Khayr brought him to the Messenger of God in Arqam's home. Upon seeing God's Messenger well, Abu Bakr was relieved. They embraced. God's Messenger was very sad as he cared very much about his best friend. But Abu Bakr did not want the Prophet to be sad. So he kept saying "I am fine, I am fine."

THE ADDRESS OF THE LAST PROPHET

God's Messenger addressed the people and said: "God let one of his men to choose a place and he chose to reach God."

When Abu Bakr heard this sentence, he began to cry. Everybody was surprised because of his crying. Because none of them could understand that the Prophet would die soon but only Abu Bakr, and that's why he was crying.

The Prophet went on his speech and said that he certainly trust Abu Bakr. He was his closest friend after God. He wished Abu Bakr peace and health. He added that if a Muslim performs the ritual prayers of Islam regularly, he or she has comfort in the Hereafter and spectacular reward.

WATCHMAN OF FRUIT GARDEN

Ibrahim ibn Adham explained that his father was one of Balkh sovereigns: "One day I went hunting with his horse. I was chasing a fox or a rabbit. I heard a noise '*O Ibrahim, you were not created and ordered for this!*' I looked around but I could not see anyone. I heard the same noise twice. I began to think that this is a warning from God. I went to one of my father's shepherds. I took his clothes and I left mine to him. I went days and nights, and arrived to Iraq. I worked as a worker for a long time. But I was worried about *halal* (right) profit. Some people advised me to go to Damascus and Tarsus to gain right profit. I went to Tarsus and worked as a watchman in a fruit garden. One day the friends of the owner of the garden came to the garden and they wanted me to bring some delicious pomegranates from the garden. I took some pomegranates. The visitors found them sour and said that 'You are waiting this garden and you always eat these pomegranates and you cannot choose sweet pomegranates!'

I said that I swear that I did not eat any pomegranate from this garden. The man said that it was a great surprise. Whoever heard this event came to see me. The garden was full of visitors. I hid myself and ran away from there."

MY SULTAN, TAKE MY VIOLETS AND GIVE MY ROSE

Samime was sitting on the sofa and reading a newspaper. The door opened and a cat came in and sat near the stove. The room was full of gloomy weather because the man of the house was in Tripoli for war. Afterwards in a blue dress and black belt a woman named Aisha came into the house. She always came and was a good friend of Samime. Her father and her fiancé Tosun was in Tripoli for war too. Aisha had a strange fortune. Her family took a letter from Istanbul and Benghazi that said they will go to Yemen. But Aisha did not receive any letter for the last six months. Her relatives had taken her to Commander Tugrul's house to stay. Commander Tugrul promised her to bring news from her father and her fiancé

Tosun. After the war, he would take them to her. Samime and Aisha were sharing the same misfortune. After Commander Tugrul went abroad, Aisha was called "little Aisha" and Samime was called "my lady." Samime was naming his husband "my rose" and naming Tosun "your rose."

They were reading newspaper about the war. In the newspaper it was saying that thirteen soldiers were fighting against a troop and twelve of them became martyr and Sergeant Mehmet fought four hours more and at the end he died by bombs.

Aisha said: "I think he is my father," and then she fainted. Samime removed her to the bed and helped her to recover. After Aisha recovered, she said that her father always wanted to die in the war and it happened.

Samime said: "I hope it was not your father. If it is so, how nice for your father has become a martyr and you have become an orphan. We must pray for our victory."

Samime's husband was also in the same danger. She was very sad. They began to cry and pray silently.

"O Aisha, my grandfather had said that my father also died in a war. They are all sacrifices of this country. This country is being watered with their blood. But I do not understand how these roses bloom white and daisies yellow. Everywhere is full of gloomy weather. Let's go to bed and have a rest my dear. Your father is with God. Maybe God forgives your rose. Maybe you will find him as a *ghazi* (war veteran)."

Aisha went to her bedroom and read a section of the Qur'an for his father's soul. She could not sleep until the morning. When she slept, she had a dream.

In her dream an angel called Love took her to Tripoli. It left Aisha in the center of a desert. In a short time her father and her fiancé Tosun came. He father kissed his daughter and said: "Here is your fiancé Tosun, I cannot come with you without driving away the enemies. Take your fiancé away Tosun." Then her father disappeared. They embraced each other and Aisha began to cry. Aisha said to her fiancé: "Either I stay with you here or I take you away."

Tosun smiled and said: "While my friends are fighting here with the enemy, how can I come with you?" Poor Aisha was crying like a pearl, but her tears were the real pearls. She said: "I spend these pearls for you." At that time Tosun opened his chest and showed diamonds on it.

Tosun said: "You should give flowers for me. If I am not a martyr, you must give the flowers to the sultan."

At that time the war was going on and they were feeling the horror of the war. They were hearing all the talking of soldiers. The soldiers were saying: "Paradise is in front of us, the Ka'ba is on our right, and God is all around us. Let's go forward."

Tosun slowly left his fiancé Aisha, and kissed her forehead, and asked her to pray for him.

When Aisha opened her eyes she was very tired because of the dream. She then remembered that if she collects some violets and gives them to the sultan, maybe the sultan will let Tosun leave military. After these thoughts she went down and began to collect violets. She would then go to the palace and say to the sultan, "Take my violets and give my rose (Tosun)." She was worried that maybe the sultan would not accept her offer. She thought that God Almighty will help her. When she arrived, she got excited. Hundreds of soldiers were walking in front of her.

She thought one of the soldiers was Tosun. She called out to him but he did not respond. She could not endure this and she fainted on the mud. Some soldiers helped her. Her violets are all in the mud. At that time Aisha remembered Tosun's speech: "If you give the flowers, it means I am alive." Aisha understood that Tosun was dead.

THE MAJOR AND MINOR PILGRIMAGE

FROM THE QUR'AN

Behold, the first House (of Prayer) established for humankind is the one at Bakkah (Makkah), a blessed place and a (center or focus of) guidance for all peoples. In it there are clear signs (demonstrating that it is a blessed sanctuary, chosen by God as the center of guidance), and the Station of Abraham. Whoever enters it is in security (against attack and fear). Pilgrimage to the House is a duty owed to God by all who can afford a way to it. And whoever refuses (the obligation of the Pilgrimage) or is ungrateful to God (by not fulfilling this command), God is absolutely independent of all creatures. (Al-Imran, 3:96-97).

(The hills of) as-Safa and Marwah are among the emblems God has appointed (to represent Islam and the Muslim community). Hence whoever does the Hajj (the Major Pilgrimage) to the House (of God, the Ka'bah) or the 'Umrah (the Minor Pilgrimage), there is no blame on him to run between them (and let them run after they go round the Ka'bah as an obligatory rite). And whoever does a good work voluntarily (such as additional going-round the Ka'bah and running between as-Safa and Marwah, and other kinds of good works) surely God is All-Responsive to thankfulness, All-Knowing. (Al-Baqarah, 2:158).

FROM THE LAST MESSENGER

Invitation

The Prophet said: "If you visit the Ka'ba and perform jihad (striving in God's cause and for humanity's good), you will become the envoy of God. Because God invited you to do those things and you obeyed His desire. God will certainly give what you want from Him."

Circumambulation of the Ka'ba

The Messenger of God said: "Circumambulation of the Ka'ba is an important worship like the daily prayers. While doing it, talk right things."

The Most Beneficial Water

The last Prophet said: "The most beneficial water is zamzam. It is a relieving cure for patients. For whatever reason it is drunk, it gives a cure for it."

THE MOST IMPORTANT WORSHIP OF WOMEN

One day Aisha asked the Messenger of God: "O Messenger of God, we know that the most important worship is *jihad*. Do we have to perform *jihad* as women?"

God's Messenger replied: "For women the most important worship is *Hajj* (pilgrimage to Mecca)."

DRINKING *ZAMZAM*

I was sitting with Ibn Abbas when another man came. Ibn Abbas asked him where he was coming from.

The man said: "I came from the *zamzam* source."

Ibn Abbas asked: "Have you drunk it as it was required?"

The man asked: "How could I do this?"

Ibn Abbas explained: "While drinking *zamzam*, turn to the *Qibla* (the direction of Mecca) and say *Bismillah* (In the Name of God). After you drink it, thank God. Because the Messenger said that the difference between Muslims and unbelievers is that unbelievers do not drink *zamzam* with desire."

MY BROTHER

Umar missed the Ka'ba very much and a great desire arose in him to visit Mecca and the Ka'ba. He demanded permission from the Messenger of God. He allowed and said: "My brother, pray for me, too."

Umar was profoundly affected by his words. Umar loved the Messenger so much. When this wonderful memory fell into his mind, so did the tears on Umar's face.

THE FEAR OF SATAN

While one of the religious men was praying in the Ka'ba, he saw Satan in a bad situation and crying. The man asked Satan why he was crying.

He said: "There were a lot of Muslims here and their aim was to pray merely for God. I am frightened of their praying."

The religious man asked: "Why are you so tired?"

The Satan said: "Because Muslims help each other and pray sincerely. Also they want to die with a real faith. But I want them die without faith. All these make me tired."

THE IMPORTANCE OF SUPPORT

If it is aimed to reach a target comfortably, easily and in security; supporting and helping are important things for everyone. This can be everywhere, for instance in the sky. What do I mean? Of course I mean the goose that fly in a V shape.

While migrating they never leave themselves alone and fly together. First they make a V shape in the sky and begin to fly. So an air flow happens from the front to the back. The goose at the back flies comfortably. So they fly twice the long distance with the same energy. If one of them leaves from the group and tries to fly alone, it has difficulty flying. It is not possible for a goose to complete the migration alone.

While flying in a V shape they often change their places. When the front gooses get tired, they go to back and the goose near the front becomes leader. So every goose in the group takes a place in every point of the group and they spend the same energy.

If one of the gooses gets ill, two gooses stay with it and wait until it gets well. If they do not lose too much time, they try to reach their own group. But if they lose much time, they find another group and join them. The new group never asks them "Why do you join us."

DAILY PRAYERS AND THE KA'BA

Think of a rose. It has little red parts and a black tuft in the middle of it. It is always fresh. Like this, Mecca and Ka'ba is like a rose with black fabric on it. Around the Ka'ba, people always pray and bend to the Ka'ba like parts of rose. Even thinking this is a wonderful thing.

JUSTICE, CHASTITY AND MODESTY

FROM THE QUR'AN

And of those whom We have created there are people who, (in due recognition of God with His Names,) guide by the truth (by God's leave) and dispense justice by it. (Al-A'raf, 7:181).

O you who believe! Be upholders and standard-bearers of right for God's sake, being witnesses for (the establishment of) absolute justice. And by no means let your detestation for a people (or their detestation for you) move you to (commit the sin of) deviating from justice. Be just: this is nearer and more suited to righteousness and piety. Seek righteousness and piety and always act in reverence for God. Surely God is fully aware of all that you do. (Al-Maidah, 5:8).

Recite and convey to them what is revealed to you of the Book, and establish the Prayer in conformity with its conditions. Surely, the Prayer restrains from all that is indecent and shameful, and all that is evil. Surely God's remembrance is the greatest (of all types of worship and not restricted to the Prayer). God knows all that you do. (Al-Ankabut, 29:45).

FROM THE LAST MESSENGER

Islamic Morality

God's Messenger said: "Each religion has a morality and the morality of Islam is *haya* (modesty, bashfulness)."

He said: "Bad manners and rudeness make everything nasty but morals makes everything acceptable."

The Messenger of God said: "If a person controls his or her anger, he or she will certainly have good deeds."

ALLAH GAVE ME MORE

There was a religious young boy in the time of Umar. He usually went to mosque to pray. Umar loved him very much. There was a woman in the young boy's neighborhood. She fell in love with the young boy. While he was going and coming from the mosque, she tried to stop him. First he was not interested in her but one day he accepted her invitation. While he was coming in to her house he began to read the following verse spontaneously: *"Those who keep from disobedience to God in reverence for Him and piety: When a suggestion from Satan touches them—they are alert and remember God, and then they have clear discernment."* (A'raf, 7:201).

After he read this verse, he fainted in front of her house door. The woman called her servant and took the young boy to his father's house. When the young boy recovered, his father asked what happened. First the young boy did not tell anything. When his father insisted, he told everything. His father asked which verse he read. The young boy recited the verse and again he fainted. But this time the young boy died. He was buried in the evening. After a day passed, this event was told to Umar. He asked why no one had told him about this incident. They said that they did not want to bother him in the evening.

Umar wanted to visit the young's grave. When they arrived there Umar read: *"But for him who lives in awe of his Lord and of the standing before his Lord (in the Hereafter), there will be two Gardens."* (Ar-Rahman, 55:46).

The young boy answered from the grave *"O Umar! God bestowed me more."*

THANKS TO ALLAH

Musa ibn abu-Isa narrated that one day Umar went to a well. He saw Ibn Maslama there. Umar asked him how he found his administration.

Muhammad ibn Maslama answered: "I think you are a successful and just administrator. You collect the tax successfully and deliver equitably. If you do not do like this, we will show you the right way."

Upon this talk, Umar said: "You say if I do wrong things you will punish me. I thank God because I am the leader of these people who correct me when I do wrong."

JUSTICE AND HUMILITY

Amawi administrator Umar ibn Abd al-Aziz was very sensitive about human rights. There were two oil lamps in his room. He was using one of them for his special life and the other for state and folk works. He was so poor that he had only one shirt.

One day while he was talking with his guest, the oil lamp went out. The guest wanted to call the servant to bring some oil for it but he did not accept his offer and said that I do not pay him extra payment for this.

So the guest tried to do it himself.

Umar ibn Abd al-Aziz did not accept this, too. He stood up and brought some oil for the oil lamp. He said that when I stood up and worked I was Umar. I sat down here and I was the same Umar.

He worked as an administrator for about three years. He had a great sense of justice just like his grandfather, Umar. Umar ibn Abd al-Aziz was poisoned at the age of forty by one of his servants. The assassin servant earned one thousand dinar for this conspiracy. When the servant admitted his crime, Umar ibn Abd al-Aziz took the money and put it into the national treasure. Then he forgave the servant and said to him "Go away from here otherwise you will be killed because of this crime."

AUNT NAKIYE

It was one of the warm August evenings. I visited aunt Nakiye in Erenköy (in Istanbul). She was sitting on the sofa under a big tree. When I arrived there, she was praying to God. I kissed her hands and sat down next to her. She prayed for me, and wished a good life for me. When I see her, I usually kiss her hands and she says the same things. After I sat down, I looked at her face and saw how old she was. There were no teeth in her mouth.

Aunt Nakiye was one my father's relatives. She was from Mora but she lived all her life in Bursa. She sent her sons to the army. She loved soldiers and military service. The most favorite activity of hers was watching the walking of soldiers in Kabataş on Fridays.

She always greeted them and gave them several gifts and food. She asked me if the Selimiye Barracks is far away from here or not. After she asked this, she looked to the sky and began to cry silently. I asked her why she asked about the Selimiye Barracks and she said nothing. Three sons of hers were martyrs. While she was crying, she was certainly thinking of her sons. She was sitting like an angel in front of me. I asked her if she was thinking of her sons or not. She said that she was and then began to talk:

"It was a summer holiday like this. I went to barracks to ask for my son Hüseyin. An officer said that my son would come soon. While I was leaving, another soldier said that my son had died and become martyr in the war. When I heard this I did not cry.

Because while I was suckling him, my husband used to say that our sons would be either *ghazi* or martyr. I have nothing in the world but three martyrs waiting for me in the other world. My son in law went to the front with his own will. After he died, my daughter cried very much. She got upset so deeply that she died three months later."

Aunt Nakiye went on talking and said: "My three sons were shot from their foreheads and chests. My dear son Hasan, he was a hero. One day Hasan said to me, 'If I was shot from my back, do not pray for me.' When I close my eyes I remember his injured body."

Aunt Nakiye prayed for me again and took a letter from her chest. It was Hasan's last letter for his father and mother: "My dear father and mother, first I kiss your hands and give my regards to all people who worry about me. I must explain something in this letter. In fact it is good news according to our religion. Especially as my father always wants, your son became martyr three days ago. I wish God forgives him. While dying I was with him. He wanted you to forgive your rights over him. He was shot with two bullets from his chest. I dug his grave and put him into the grave with my own hands. He was smiling. While fighting with the enemy violently, your son became martyr. The enemy was coming on us like a black cloud. At the beginning our captain became a martyr and then our sergeant. At that time your son Hasan took the flag and began to run to the enemy saying 'Allah Allah.' I wish you saw him at that time. The enemy returned and attacked for the last time and at that time Hasan became a martyr. At the end we won the war. When I went to him, he opened his eyes and looked at me for the last time.

My father always said that I am a son of martyr and I want to be a father of martyr. So my father's prayers were accepted. As I know a new attack will begin. Pray for me. I kiss your hands.

Your son, Hüseyin.

It was a gloomy weather. I looked at aunt Nakiye's face. She was thinking and looking to the sky constantly. I wanted to give the letter back. She wanted me to read it again but I could not.

As Hüseyin's friends explained when they returned to Istanbul, Hüseyin was taken prisoner. In the prison Hüseyin and his friends attacked the watchman and fired ammunition. At that time he was injured. While running away he had to jump into a river and the following day his corpse was found. Namely with the help of Hüseyin all friends escaped and participated in their army.

I stood up and kissed aunt Nakiye's hands.

Three years passed and aunt Nakiye was very ill. In her house there was a deep silence. Aunt Nakiye died in this silence. Funeral prayers were performed in the mosque. There were a lot of soldiers in the funeral. When we reached Kabataş, two groups of soldiers welcomed us. It was the last duty for a mother who has three martyr sons.

AHMET HİKMET MÜFTÜOĞLU
JULY 17, 1895